Hunting with Spaniels

TRAINING YOUR FLUSHING DOG

By Paul Morrison

COUNTRY DOGS™ SERIES

Kennel Club Books®
A Division of BowTie, Inc.

EDITORIAL

Andrew DePrisco *Editor-in-Chief*
Amy Deputato *Senior Editor*
Jamie Quirk *Editor*

ART

Sherise Buhagiar *Senior Graphic Artist*
Bill Jonas *Book Design*
Joanne Muzyka *Digital Imaging*

The publisher would like to thank the following photographers for their contributions to this book: Mary Bloom, David Dalton, Tara Darling, Isabelle Francais, Carol Ann Johnson, Paul and Lynn Morrison, Philippe Roca, Alice van Kempen, and Haja van Wessem.

Cover photos by Philippe Roca.

Kennel Club Books® Country Dogs™ Series
Hunting with Spaniels
Copyright © 2009

A Division of BowTie, Inc.

40 Broad Street, Freehold, NJ 07728 • USA

Library of Congress Cataloging-in-Publication Data

Morrison, Paul, 1955–
  Hunting with spaniels / by Paul Morrison.
      p. cm. — (Country dog series)
  Includes bibliographical references.
  ISBN 978-1-59378-729-5
  1. Spaniels—Training. 2. Hunting dogs—Training. I. Title.
  SF429.S7M67 2008
  636.752'435—dc22
                        2008033755

Printed and bound in China

15 14 13 12 11 10 09   1 2 3 4 5 6 7 8 9 10

Contents

Paul and Lynn Morrison with two of their
American Water Spaniels.

Introduction

It has been more than twenty years since I entered the land of the flushing spaniel and discovered what I believe to be the quintessential type of field dog. At the time, I was not necessarily looking for a flushing dog; I simply wanted a versatile dog that would be all I needed in a gundog, rolled into one tidy package. I did not begin my search looking for a single breed or a single type of dog; in fact, just the opposite was the case. You see, I have never specialized in any particular type of hunting but simply in the sport of hunting, and I like it that way.

What I hunt is predicated not on what my friends hunt or what type of hunting is most prevalent in my area but on the type of quarry available on any given day. I needed then, as I do now, a dog or dogs that would make it possible for me to successfully hunt that quarry and return home with a full game bag. As an upland enthusiast, I sought a dog that would have a keen nose, good speed, and boldness and not be too much trouble to clean up following a day spent in the swales and underbrush of the nearby coverts. As a waterfowl hunter, I

needed a dog that loved to retrieve. Such a dog would sit comfortably on a cold and blustery day, calmly waiting for the next opportunity to fetch a duck from the marsh and retrieve it gently to hand. To my way of thinking, I needed two dogs—one a pointer and the other a retriever. My wife's way of thinking, however, was that two dogs were going to be one dog too many, and well, her way of thinking was, of course, more correct than mine.

When my search began, not only was I looking for one dog more than I was allowed (I mean, one more dog than I needed) but I also was seeking something that would be far too big for a house dog. You see, I had assumed that since I was no hunting specialist, I would need two dogs, as this would allow me to cover all bases and have the best dog for each situation, land and water. I had been considering the usual suspects: a nice Labrador that would be more than enough dog for my waterfowl hunting and could, if called upon, perform adequately in the uplands; and a good performing Brittany that would tear up the pheasant fields or grouse woods while showing some versatility as a retriever. This was my idea of the ideal combination. When reality set in, though, it became apparent that my game plan had to change. So, with a new understanding of the course I would have to take, I returned to the books, the magazines, and the conversations with other hunters, which I hoped would eventually lead me to the ideal dog.

Surprisingly, it was my wife, Lynn, not me, who found the ideal dog. She had been told of a breed that excelled at retrieving and flushing and had a long, albeit obscure, history of hunting—the American Water Spaniel. Her suggestion that I look into that breed led to the usual spousal skepticism, followed by a great deal of research on my part as I tried to prove that she had been led astray and that I knew best.

My skepticism centered not only on the particular breed in question, which was little known and difficult to find but also on spaniels in general. A spaniel for hunting? I had never run into a spaniel while grouse or pheasant hunting around Michigan, and I certainly had never seen a spaniel around the marshes while duck and goose hunting. Why in the world would I consider a spaniel? Undoubtedly, this was going to be a short detour on my path to the ideal dog. Well, not so fast! My research turned up not only a good amount of information on the American Water Spaniel in particular but an overwhelming amount of information on spaniels in general.

I came to learn that spaniels are not specialists, in the sense that they primarily either locate game or retrieve shot birds, but jacks of all trades, performing both functions equally well. In short, they are much like me and probably many other hunters, who lean toward hunting whatever game provides the best opportunity on a given day. The hunter who goes out one day to push through the corn stubble and fence rows in pursuit of a clever old rooster pheasant and then spends the next day looking out across a few dozen decoys is probably best served by having a spaniel as a hunting partner. The guy or gal who likes to walk the edges of a beaver pond for grouse and needs a dog that will retrieve a bird from the water as quickly and easily as he will from land is probably best served by having a spaniel as a hunting partner. And the hunter who likes to occasionally test his skill at putting a rabbit or two in the game bag will find the spaniel a truly versatile companion. Add to all of that the fact that most spaniels are compact enough to take up only a little room on the couch as they curl up next to you, and you really begin to wonder why do we not see and read more about these great little dogs.

When it comes to hunting dogs, the flushing spaniel is about the least popular of the three basic types: pointers/setters, retrievers, and spaniels. This is borne out by a variety of numbers provided by the American Kennel Club (AKC). For instance, if you add up all of the spaniel pups registered with the AKC in any given year and compare that number with the number of retriever pups or pointer and setter pups, you will see that the spaniels finish a distant third. If you look at the number of field events, both hunt tests and field trials, run each year for spaniels and compare it with the number of such events held for either retrievers or pointers and setters, you will see that the spaniels are, once again, least popular. The question is, why?

Every time I see how relatively easy it is for spaniel trainers to mold these little dogs into solid hunting dogs, I wonder why so many other people are driving themselves mad with frustration as they work with other breeds, trying to fashion the perfect hunting dog by electronic and other means. After twenty years in spaniels, I have come to the conclusion that they resist spaniels for the following reasons.

First, there is the propaganda. Although a diligent search of magazines and books will turn up nostalgic musings of great hunts conducted with the aid of a spaniel or of great spaniels that won field trial after field trial, the number of stories about spaniel hunts and winners will probably never be comparable to those found about retrievers, pointers, and setters. If you pick up a hunting-dog magazine, you are far more likely to read of an English Setter coming to a stylish point as it locks on to a partridge in some far-off northern hardwood forest or to see pictures of a pointer working in front of a wagon on a southern plantation quail hunt. What waterfowl magazine does not contain a story (or two or three) of a Labrador Retriever making the nearly impossible retrieve? We hunters grow up with such propaganda, and we come to expect that the best grouse dog is an English Setter or the best retriever is a Labrador.

Such beliefs do have merit, but they are very narrow-minded. The spaniels make exceptional hunting dogs too, and the stories told by the owners of these dogs can bring as many goosebumps and dreams of glory as can those with which we are all so much more familiar. Perhaps if we spaniel enthusiasts would step forward to write such stories and if publishers would be willing to print more of them, we would see a surge in the recognition of these awesome hunting machines. Maybe if more people would read about the little spaniel that trailed a running rooster pheasant through a thick stand of cattails, down into a wet slough, and up into a patch of wheat stubble as it put the bird to flight, we would see more hunters with spaniels. Perhaps if we would see more pictures of that little spaniel returning with the pheasant gently but firmly held in his mouth as he leaps high over a fence to return quickly and dutifully to his owner, we would see more hunters afield with spaniels. In short, if the spaniel community would do a better job of promoting its own, perhaps these merry little dogs would get greater respect and recognition within the hunting community.

Another reason I think the spaniels get short shrift is because of the structure of the field trial programs established for spaniels. Many writers routinely claim that if you don't buy a dog bred from field trial stock, you simply cannot get a good hunting spaniel. Those who read such statements come to believe that these experts are right. What the writers fail to mention, though, is that unlike the pointing dog and retriever communities, which have field trial programs open to all varieties, the spaniel world's U.S. field trial program is breed specific. Whether born of necessity or simply a product of breed prejudice, there are only three spaniel breeds (Cocker Spaniels, English Cocker Spaniels, and English Springer Spaniels) that offer a field trial program, which leaves the other six breeds without one. Although this situation appears to limit the availability of good hunting spaniels, the truth is that there are plenty of spaniels that produce solid field dogs, and they do not come from field trial backgrounds or even have field trials available to them. Of course, you still have to do your research to find a good pup, and those whose sires or dams have field trial or hunt test backgrounds certainly have better odds of being successful hunting dogs. Just don't write off a spaniel pup entirely because it happens to possess a less than stellar pedigree.

Since the mid 1980s, the AKC has offered a hunt test program that provides field titles to all of the recognized flushing spaniel breeds. There will be more on this program later in the book. Here I want to be sure to mention that, for the average hunter, the titles earned at the mid- and upper levels of this program point toward a dog that has the ability to perform well in the field and, one hopes, to reproduce that ability in his offspring. The AKC hunt test program is a good substitute for showcasing the field dogs and helping determine where a person may be able to obtain a sound hunting companion.

Finally, another reason the spaniel ranks lowest on the list is one of perception of its temperament. The frequency with which I have had to field questions regarding the hyper spaniel, the nippy spaniel, or the moody spaniel is just too great to mention. Are they hyper? Some are, but many are not. Do they nip? Sure, some do, but most do not. Moody? Well, I would not label most spaniels as laid-back and easygoing, but they did not get the reputation of being merry dogs because they are temperamental. Spaniels are dogs, and all dogs have their drawbacks from time to time. What I have seen in the spaniels I have known, especially those bred primarily for hunting, is that most are fiercely loyal, loving dogs, with an uncanny ability and desire to go after anything and everything they are asked to hunt. If we spaniel enthusiasts could ingrain that one understanding into the minds of every hunter we meet, there might be a newfound appreciation for these little dogs, and they might gain a few more fans within the hunting community.

Of course, it is likely that you are already a fan of the flushing spaniel or you probably would not have picked up this book. So why mention all of these comparative ramblings about the types of hunting dogs and my thoughts on the flushing spaniel's place in this grand scheme? As a spaniel enthusiast, I hope that you want to do your best to showcase not only your dog but all spaniels to whatever circles you travel in. Whether your world is one shared with your hunting partners or is one that includes other spaniel enthusiasts and the field games they may play, I believe it to be in the best interest of the dogs and sport we love that we produce a decent if not great hunting companion.

This book is written to help you develop your dog into a truly efficient and cooperative flushing dog. It is hoped that the information shared within these pages and the techniques found herein will serve you well as you partner with your dog and slowly but deliberately turn him into a "hunt'n machine." Remember that every journey begins by placing one foot in front of the other, and the reward of the trip is not necessarily its completion but the journey itself. I hope that you enjoy this process, but most of all I hope that you enjoy your dog.

A hunting spaniel is an efficient worker in a
medium-size package with the potential to
flush and retrieve with the best of 'em.

Chapter

1

What Makes a Spaniel a Spaniel?

Ask the average gundog fan just what makes a retriever a retriever, and you will probably get a very quick answer that goes something like this: "Why heck, it's the retrieving! You know there is no better dog out there at fetching game than a retriever. That's what they are bred for, you know—fetching up them birds." Just as their name implies, that is what retrievers are all about, and a few do a passable job at finding and flushing birds as well.

It is no different with the pointers and setters. Although there is sometimes a bit of puzzlement over the term *setter*, most gundog folks know that these dogs point their game. A few show some versatility by doing an adequate job of retrieving shot game as well, but once again, their name indicates what they do best. So we have retrievers that retrieve and pointers that point. But what exactly does the term *spaniel* tell us about this type of gundog?

The truth is, not a whole lot. You don't really become familiar with the essence of these dogs until you get to know one or you read a bit about them. If you are going to train a spaniel, you need to have a sense of what this type of dog is about and

The Field Spaniel is a compact dog, often with a playful demeanor, who's a tireless worker on all types of terrain and in water.

The Welsh Springer Spaniel is a friendly, lively dog with plenty of energy and endurance for fieldwork.

what your expectations should be. So let's take some time to explore what it means to be a spaniel.

With some nine recognized varieties of hunting spaniels found in the United States, each with its own unique qualities, trying to reduce the spaniel to a narrow description is nigh on to impossible. However, despite the diverse physical attributes of the various spaniels, they all possess one primary tendency in their hunting skills: they all flush the bird rather than point it. How these differing breeds put the bird to flight ranges from the hard-driving flush of a field-bred English Springer to the slower, more deliberate flush common to some of the other spaniels. If you like to witness what might be best described as colorful conversation, just ask a group of spaniel owners, each with a different breed, which is the correct type of flush and then stand back. After the dust begins to settle a bit, someone will finally bring out the correct answer: the best flush is the one that is right for the breed in question. In 2007, the American Kennel Club began compiling a description of each spaniel breed's hunting style as described by its parent club. You can obtain that information by contacting the AKC or searching for it on their Web site, www.akc.org.

Before a dog gets the opportunity to flush a bird, though, he must have the ability to find one. For this he will need a good nose coupled with what we often call drive but may be better stated as desire. I do not believe that there is any type of gundog better at using its nose and locating game than a spaniel. I have watched many spaniels locate bird scent from dozens of yards away and take a straight line directly to the bird to produce it for the gun. I have seen dogs whose heads snapped so quickly from one direction to another after coming across scent that I was surprised they did not hurt themselves. Time after time I have seen spaniels root out birds from brush piles, bramble thickets, and blown-down stands of grass, when I would have sworn that there could not possibly be a bird anywhere nearby. Isn't that what all of us hunters are after—a dog whose nose is far superior to ours and who knows how to use it? No matter what variety of spaniel you own or are considering, the one you get will probably possess a good to exceptional nose.

Unfortunately, not all spaniels have the desire to work a field and pursue game that they should have, and consequently one cannot say that all spaniels are or can be hunting spaniels. Some dogs just do not seem to have that little spark that makes them hit a field with panache. Those who do are a marvel to behold. Spaniels seem to have an instinctive propensity for quartering a field that makes them a more efficient workhorse than the dog that takes a straight line down a field or runs hell-bent for leather hither and yon, with no set purpose in mind. Although the spaniel trainer will work to mold this instinct to fit his needs, it is nice to know that the foundation for this behavior is a natural one.

As was noted earlier, a key component in a spaniel's overall attributes is his willingness and desire to retrieve. Perhaps it comes from the spaniel's often-noted propensity toward a cooperative nature, or maybe it is because spaniels tend to bond so quickly with their human partners that they just naturally want to bring everything they find back to their masters. Whatever the reason, the spaniel's desire to retrieve is one of the common characteristics that make it a desirable hunting dog for the average American hunter, especially a hunter who is limited to one small- to medium-sized dog at a time. This particular quality is so strong that spaniels take to water about as well as any of the retrievers. In fact, so important is the retrieving work—both on land and in the water—for a spaniel that it is a main factor in AKC spaniel hunt tests. The dog that will not readily retrieve either from the water or on the land will not and should not qualify in a hunting test.

What makes a spaniel a spaniel? Well, it is not that it flushes birds, has a good nose, or retrieves. It is that the spaniel bears all of those attributes in one neat little package and performs them all very well. The essence of the hunting spaniel is that it possesses all of these distinctive qualities and through its cooperative spirit allows us to mold those qualities in a way that gives us an excellent working companion. The work of a spaniel cannot be described in one word (such as *retrieve* or *point*) because its talents are too numerous.

Cocker Spaniels (both American and English, the latter of which is shown here) tend to have a reputation as show dogs, but don't count out their talents in the field.

Versatility is a key component of the working spaniel, as demonstrated by this enthusiastically leaping English Springer Spaniel.

What characteristics do you want in a spaniel? The Clumber Spaniel is a deliberate worker, known for his excellent tracking skills.

Where to Find a Hunting Spaniel

You have decided that your new hunting companion is going to be a spaniel, and now you need to find a good one. Where do you start? Well, let's talk first about where not to look. Put down that newspaper—never, ever, consider it as a source for quality gundogs. It doesn't matter one bit if your best buddy got his top-performing hunting dog from some obscure newspaper ad; if he did, he was very lucky, and you can't count on luck. If you could, you would have won the lottery by now. If you want a quality gundog who will be a companion for ten or more years, work all day without breaking down, and train well, you are going to have to do some research.

Each breed recognized by the American Kennel Club (AKC) has a parent club affiliated with the AKC. This is the club that is primarily responsible for and represents the specific breed within the AKC. (For instance, the English Springer Spaniel Field Trial Association, Inc., is the AKC parent club of the English Springer Spaniel.) Most of the parent clubs have a breeder referral service and will assist you in locating breeders.

Start by finding reputable breeders with field-bred lines. Visit the breeders, meet the puppies, and gather all of the information that you can.

By contacting the club's secretary, you can get either a list of breeders or the name of the person who can supply it to you. Most clubs have Web sites on which they offer the contact information of their breeder referral people, or they may actually have their lists of breeders readily available online. A list of club-affiliated breeders is a good starting point for your search, but keep in mind that not all breeders are gundog breeders, as some concentrate on show dogs with less emphasis on working qualities. Be sure to ask the right questions when you call or write the breeders who interest you.

The Internet is now one of the greatest tools for locating dog breeders. A simple search will turn up an assortment of breeders for any given breed, and many of them will indicate on their Web sites the type of dogs (hunting, show, companion, and so on) that they are breeding. A good Web site will also provide pictures, pedigrees, health, and contact information that will aid you in your search and may be invaluable. As with all advertising (yes, Web sites are just another form of advertising), you will need to filter through the clutter and get to the heart of the matter to be sure that the person behind the site is a reputable one. The best way to research this is to get on the phone and call those breeders who seem to have that which you seek—a field-bred pup.

Working with a Breeder

Once on the phone with the breeder, you are going to have to become the investigator to learn exactly what it is this breeder may have available and how that fits into your search criteria. A good breeder will also be investigating you by asking detailed questions about your expectations, home situation, and history with dogs. Such a breeder is not looking for a puppy buyer as much as he is looking for a loving and lifelong home for his puppy. Be prepared to answer questions sincerely, because sincerity will help to ensure that, rather than simply "ending up" with a puppy, you get the proper puppy for your situation.

When considering a gundog breeder, you should look for one who has both the experience and the willingness to work with any training problems that may creep up as your puppy matures. Although it is not imperative for you to find a breeder who is also a trainer, the benefits that come from doing so can be well worth the extra effort it may take to locate such a person. This type of breeder need not be, and probably will not be, a professional, but simply a knowledgeable amateur with a good track record. Experienced breeder-trainers have likely seen any problem you may run into with your puppy and can help you get over the little humps in your training regimen. So if you find such a person whom you like and whose dogs seem to have what you want in a puppy, consider yourself fortunate if he is willing to place one of his pups in your hands.

Another advantage of dealing with breeder-trainers is that they sometimes have started or finished dogs for sale. Although this book is intended to help you train your own dog, it would be inappropriate to ignore the fact that not everyone is capable of or interested in doing so. Such people will benefit from the purchase of a started or finished dog. The problem is that exactly what those terms mean is left up to interpretation. So if a breeder offers to sell you such a dog, clarify just what it is that the dog is trained to do. If you believe that the cost to purchase a dog like this is worth the extra money (the more training he has, the higher the price) and you have proof that the dog does indeed do what the breeder says, then, by all means, feel comfortable in your decision to go forward.

Flying feathers attract this young English Springer's interest.

Word of mouth about where to find a good pup is as beneficial today as it ever was, but to hear about a great litter or a potentially good gundog pup, you need to be in the right circles. So start attending a few hunt tests, field trials, or your local spaniel club's field training events. By doing this, you will have the opportunity not only to hear about various litters but also to possibly see the performances of the sires or dams of those litters. Nothing will give you a greater appreciation for the work that your pup may be able to do than witnessing what his mother or father can do. Additionally, you may be able to meet the breeder face-to-face and strike up a conversation. A cordial introduction and a brief discussion about your search for a

pup is probably all you should expect at such a meeting. After all, the primary reason these folks are at events like this is not to sell pups but to work their dogs. If the breeder is interested in discussing the matter with you further, he or she will be sure to take the necessary steps.

You may also have the opportunity to talk to others who are not breeders but simply gundog owners. Such individuals will often be willing to give you their opinions about where you will find a nice pup and where you will not. Keep in mind, though, that some of these people will be harboring a few prejudices of their own, so you may have to work through those to separate the wheat from the chaff.

There are a couple of final items worth mentioning before moving on from this topic. The first involves the reading of pedigrees. As a breeder, I always chuckle a bit to myself when a person asks to see a pedigree. First of all, the reading of pedigrees, while not difficult, is really only of benefit to those who possess a thorough knowledge of the particular breed. Yes, a pedigree can show some of the titles that the pup's ancestors earned, which usually affects a buyer's decision but will not tell you the whole story. For instance, a title will not tell you how well the offspring are going to perform, whether the dog was professionally trained or trained by an owner-handler, or just how easily the dog earned the title in question. Given all the questions a pedigree leaves unanswered, one must treat it less as a definitive predictor and more as a starting point from which to gather further information. After all, many dogs with less than stellar pedigrees, that have never been entered in a hunt test or field trial let alone earned a title, have been exceptional gundogs and produced the same. But how do you know that without a title to back it up?

References! Yes, references. This is where I believe your research really needs to be focused once you have decided upon a potential litter and breeder. Ask for references and follow up on them so you can get firsthand reports on dogs that this breeder has bred. No one can tell me more about a dog or his offspring than the people who have worked with the dogs or witnessed the work they have done. More important still are references from people who actually hunt their dogs, not those who simply train them or run them in hunt tests and field trials. The average gundog enthusiast does not run his dog in such events but does hit the coverts, fence rows, and marshes each fall in search of game. The average gundog

owner does not train daily and is far from a professional. Such a person has likely not even considered paying for the service of a professional to help train his dog. Yet if the dog is a good hunting dog and possesses the qualities of a well-bred spaniel, the hunter will know it. If owners have had trouble training, controlling, or in any way getting out of their dogs what they feel they should, you will probably hear about it. Likewise, any successes they have had will be shared with you. Can these folks be a bit biased in their perception of how their dog performs? Of course, but my experience has been that they tend to be more informative than the pedigree and more down-to-earth than many breeders. Like pedigrees, references are another tool to help you make your decision.

Don't forget to talk about the health of the pup's ancestors. No dog is going to be worth his salt as a field dog if he is unable to run in the field because of hip dysplasia or cannot see well because of juvenile cataracts. Every breed has a fairly well-known set of health issues that plague it from time to time, and you will need to discover just what those are as you research the various breeds. Here again the breed's parent club may be able to help you with pertinent information. Once armed with the knowledge of a breed's health concerns, you can quiz the breeder about the steps that he has taken to make certain that his breeding dogs are free of such problems. Ask for and expect to receive proof of any health clearances and records obtained by the breeder. Any honest and concerned breeder will gladly provide you with copies of health certificates and clearance numbers to assure you that he has done all he can to make sure that the pup you receive is going to be a healthy dog. Finally, ask about a written health guarantee. In today's environment, every good breeder provides a health guarantee of some kind, which will address just what procedures will be followed in the event that the pup has a genetically-based health issue.

As you can see, finding a good pup is not all that easy and involves a lot more effort on your part than simply picking up the local paper. The process demands your commitment to quality; that commitment will improve your chances of obtaining a sound and driven hunting companion.

Picking Your Pup

OK, you have found the breeder from whom you want to buy, and the pups in the litter are ready to go to their new homes. All that is left for you to do is pick out the perfect pup. So how do you go about doing that? What tricks can you use to make certain that the pup you get will be the perfect pup for you?

I think that one of the worst things you can do is to choose your own pup. Unless you are a breeder, an expert on the breed, an expert spaniel person, or an experienced trainer—or you have some proven innate sixth sense when it comes to choosing puppies—you have no business deciding which is the right pup for your situation. Leave that up to the breeder. Why? Because having lived with and trained the litter's dam for a few years, raised these pups from birth, observed the development of their individual personalities, and, it is hoped, introduced them to bird scent, wings, loud noises, and so forth, the breeder knows these pups and is best qualified to choose a dog that is right for you. Of course, this is provided that you have given the breeder a thorough understanding of what it is you want in a hunting dog.

I always recommend that puppy buyers provide the breeder with written descriptions of what they are looking for in a pup as well as in an adult dog. Furthermore, I suggest that they tell the breeder about their particular lifestyle so the breeder can make certain that what they want is going to match their personal situations. For instance, let's say that you tell the breeder you want the most rambunctious, driven, high-energy pup in the litter because you want a fireball in the field when the dog grows up. That is fine and dandy if you are always on the go, running five miles a day, playing in the yard every night with the kids, and hiking on weekends. However, if your idea of a workout is lifting a six-pack every Saturday and Sunday while watching *Star Trek*, and you have not been out working in the back yard for more than a month, you better think twice about a high-energy pup or dog and start looking for one more suited to your personality.

How can you be sure, even when you've given the breeder all of these facts, that he is going to give you a good dog? Well, if you don't trust the breeder, why are you buying a puppy from him? The relationship you build with the breeder is one built on trust; if you can't trust him to get you a good dog, you had better look elsewhere for a pup.

There you have it. The one trick I can give you for picking out the perfect pup is don't do it. Let your breeder decide. If you are going to insist on choosing the pup yourself, then you can avail

An American Water Spaniel pup introduces himself to a decoy.

yourself of the myriad books, magazine articles, Web sites, and friends that believe in some "scientific formula" that will assure you get just the right dog. As for me, I will continue to tell hunters that no one will do as good a job at picking out the right pup as the knowledgeable breeder.

Breeders are not foolproof, but over the decades I have seen far more success from taking the breeder's advice than from any other methods of puppy selection. Are there ever errors in judgment that result in a mismatch between owner and dog? Yes, but I have seen far fewer from this method than from any other. And heck, it beats just reaching in and grabbing the first pup you can!

The crate provides a place of safe confinement and
security at home and on the road.

Chapter 3

Making a Den for Your Dog

Even the newest of the newcomers to the world of dogs has probably heard that dogs are den animals that seek small confined enclosures for both comfort and security. It is because of this basic understanding that the dog community has come to embrace, promote, and practically insist on dogs being raised with kennels or crates (the words are often used interchangeably) as their dens, be they kept as house or outside dogs. Used as a means to reduce stress, prevent unwanted behavior, housebreak a pup, or provide a measure of added safety, a dog crate can be of tremendous value to every owner. Whether you live with a dog of eight weeks, eight years, or eighteen years, a crate is an asset.

For the gundog owner, the crate becomes a traveling doghouse, one the dog is used to, providing him with a measure of normalcy and safety when on the road. In fact, if you have no crate, many dog-friendly motels suddenly become hostile to the idea of letting you keep your companion in the room with you, fearing damage done to the room. Most lodging establishments that allow dogs do so on the condition

An example of a hard-sided plastic crate, often recommended in cooler weather.

that they be crated when alone in their rooms.

Contrary to the beliefs of the few who decry the use of crates for our canine companions, the majority of dogs favor their crates over other types of confinement or no confinement at all. Even the youngest of pups, when properly introduced to it, will show an astonishing desire to use the crate for rest and security. It is for this reason that confining your dog to a crate should never be used as a form of punishment. For one, a dog

simply does not understand the concept of being "sent to his room"; for another, a dog needs a safety net where he can feel secure, and that is the crate. Taking that feeling of security away from your dog because of disciplinary measures doled out with a crate could cause your dog to exhibit further unwanted behaviors.

Where you choose to keep the crate is usually a matter of preference, but I recommend that it be near the family's primary living space as opposed to a laundry room, basement, or other out-of-the-way area. Since most spaniels are rather compact in size, their crates can often fit well in the average family room, dining area, or kitchen. It is important to note that although the crate may be kept in close proximity to the rest of the family, it is still the dog's den and should be treated with respect. When the dog is in his kennel, he should be off-limits to pestering by young children. No child should be allowed to intrude on the dog's space by crawling into his crate, no matter how cute such activity may seem to be.

Crate Types

The two most widely used crate types are metal-wire and plastic. The choice is really a matter of personal preference. In warmer weather, I like to use a metal-wire crate because of the additional airflow, but in the winter, when traveling, I prefer a plastic crate, which maintains a warmer environment for the dog and does a better job of keeping mud and debris from being deposited inside my car or truck.

SIZE MATTERS

The best crate size for your dog will depend upon his age, level of conditioning, and, of course, physical size. As an adult dog, your hunting partner will need enough room to be able to stand, stretch, and turn around comfortably in his crate. Although most kennel manufacturers provide a list of appropriate breeds for their various crate sizes, it is always best to double-check the anticipated adult size of your dog against the crate manufacturers' recommendations.

Never start a young puppy out in a crate sized for an adult dog. This will only lead to problems of crate-soiling, as the pup will learn that he can easily relieve himself at one end of the crate while staying perfectly comfortable at the other end. If this happens too often with a young pup, it can become a problem that will require a time-consuming, and often frustrating, solution.

So no matter the age of your dog, he should have a crate of appropriate size. This may mean providing your dog with as many as three different crates between early puppyhood and full physical maturity. Although this may seem a bit costly, the benefits realized from keeping the pup in the right size

A crate made of metal wire allows more air to flow through and gives the dog a full view of what's going on around him.

The time you take to accustom your spaniel to his crate pays off in a dog who finds comfort in his den, his own private retreat.

breaking problems, damaged furniture, destroyed shoes and clothing, and possibly an injured—or worse—dog that chewed or ate the wrong thing while you were away. Your pup is too valuable a companion to not provide a safe place to house him while you are away or unable to keep a close eye on him.

INSIDE TIPS

Whatever type of crate used, I like to have bedding inside for the dog's comfort, even though I find that most dogs simply push the bedding aside and lie on the bare floor. Bedding is usually not given to dogs under the age of twelve to eighteen months for two reasons. The first is that some young dogs, puppies mostly, will learn that bedding can absorb or hide their "accidents" should they urinate or defecate in the crate, and they take advantage of this, relieving themselves more frequently than necessary. The second is that young dogs need to chew as they grow, and they find that the bedding makes a wonderful chew toy, no matter how many other toys may be kept in the crate.

The crate is also used as the spot where the dog is fed. This helps keep him away from the dinner table during meals and lets

crate will be well worth the money spent. There are ways to reduce the cost of crate purchases, including shopping for puppy crates at garage sales or thrift stores and holding off on purchasing the fancy super deluxe model until maturity has been reached. There is a cost to not properly crate training your pup, a cost that is borne out in house-

him understand that the kennel is truly his den. Feed your dog at the same time that you sit down to dinner by having him go to his kennel and placing the food bowl in the kennel with him. When the family has finished with dinner, the pup can be let out of his crate.

Although I always have water available to a dog outside of the crate, this is not generally the case for a dog being kept in his crate. The obvious exception is when the temperature or other conditions warrant having an ample supply of water at hand. In any other case, too much water provided to a dog that is going to be staying in his kennel for the next eight to nine hours is asking for an accident to happen. Under most conditions, a mature dog can comfortably go as long as eight to ten hours without water.

Finally, use caution when crating your dog with a collar on. A simple buckle collar is not likely to be a problem, but choke or chain collars of any type should never be left on your dog when he is in a crate, as the collar can catch on the bars or the latch of the crate and pose a real danger.

Crate Introduction

If everything is going perfectly, then you have picked up your pup during the day and have some time to work with him before he has to spend his first night away from his littermates. This will give you time to practice all of the following steps, which begin the process of crate training on a positive note. If, however, you are taking the pup home in the evening, then try to make time to follow these steps beginning bright and early the next day.

You need to make crate training as positive for the dog as possible. If your breeder was wise and helpful, your pup probably got some introduction to a crate while still with his littermates. For instance, when I raise a litter of pups, I place a crate from which the door has been removed into the puppy pen when the pups are around six weeks old. Within hours the pups are instinctively using that crate as their place to pile up with one another and sleep. This positive association makes the transition to a crate with a door much smoother.

Let's assume that you have a good part of the day to work with your new pup and properly introduce him to a crate. Have the crate set up, with the door open, in an area where the dog will be playing and lounging with you while you are in the house.

Occasionally try to lure the pup to the crate with the use of a dog treat—make it a good one, like a small piece of a hot dog. Lure the pup into the crate by first letting him sniff the treat and then tossing the treat inside the crate. As the pup walks into the crate to get the treat, say "kennel" in a calm and matter-of-fact voice. This allows you to associate the word *kennel* with the action of the pup going into his crate, thus beginning the entire training process. Repeat this process several times throughout the day for the first few days, and your pup will quickly learn the meaning of the kennel command.

At some point you will have to begin to close the crate door and secure the pup for a while. Before you do this, it is best to make certain that the pup has done his business and will probably not have to go again for a little while. Of course, pups are not always cooperative, and if you simply must crate the pup without his having gone potty beforehand, well, do what you must. Lure the pup into his crate as you did earlier, give him some gentle praise, and toss in a toy with which he can occupy his time. If the pup has been very active prior to this, he is probably going to settle down in short order and drift off to sleep; if not, a toy will help

keep him occupied. If the crate is in the main living area and you need to leave the room, try to stay with the pup for a while before doing so. He is probably going to whine or bark a bit after first being closed in the crate, so if you are in the room, you can talk to him and attempt to reassure him. Whatever you do, do not remove him from the crate while he is barking or whining; doing so will simply begin to teach him that such behavior is all that is needed to gain his release. Your biggest challenge here is to resolve that you will not give in to your pup's whining and barking after he has first been secured in his crate. If you can stick to that plan, all will go well.

If you do not need to leave the pup secured in the crate right away, then you can take advantage of your time to slowly introduce the pup to being closed in the crate. Lure him into the crate, close the door, wait near the crate until the pup has quieted down for a short time, stay a few minutes, and then open the crate door and let him loose. Praise him for being a good little pup and, if it has been a while since he last did his business, usher him outside to let him relieve himself. If you are sure that he does not have to go outside upon his release, then allow him some free time to play before putting him back in his crate and starting the whole process over again.

As with all training, repetition helps speed the process along, so if you can take some time to work with the puppy on accustoming him to his crate several times each day for the first few days, he will quickly learn what is expected. Start with short periods of between five and ten minutes in the crate, and gradually lengthen the time to an hour or so. As was said earlier, if he falls asleep, simply let him be until he wakes up, and then get him outside—by picking him up and carrying him outside—again before allowing him freedom in the house.

Pup's First Night

Whether you have had the pup throughout the day and followed the aforementioned steps or have just arrived home from the breeder with the puppy, try to give him a good deal of playtime to tire him out before you head off to bed. Pick up his water dish about an hour before bedtime to avoid having him fill his bladder. Take him outside to relieve himself, and do your best to make certain that he has done so before putting him in the crate.

Set up a place in your bedroom where you can put the crate. I like it right next to the bed so that I can reassure the pup that I am there. If he whines, simply reach into the crate with your fingers to calm him. If he is truly tired, he will settle quickly and go to sleep; if not, you may lose a bit of sleep that night until he does. Just understand that his sleep cycle is likely to be fairly similar to yours, triggered by darkness and quiet. So turn out the lights and do your best to establish a peaceful rest area for him to relax.

Puppies are much like babies; a young one is not going to sleep through the night without having

Be careful with bedding in your pup's crate, as many youngsters like to chew on anything soft.

to do his business. In anticipation of this, you should set an alarm to go off four hours after going to bed. When the alarm sounds, get up, quickly dress, and carry the pup from the kennel right outside to potty. Once you are sure he is done, take him directly back to his kennel. Close the crate door and go back to bed. He should settle back down in short order and go to sleep; if he does not, follow the routine described earlier. At this point, the pup should be able to sleep through to morning.

One of the benefits of having the pup's crate next to the bed or at least in the same room with you is that you can hear the pup if he fusses during the night, indicating that he has to potty. When this happens, quickly get the pup outside and follow the aforementioned routine. If the puppy should happen to relieve himself in his crate, do not reprimand him. The fault likely lies with you, not the puppy (maybe you did not set the alarm or did not make certain that he had relieved himself before going to bed). In any case, he is not going to understand what it is he is being scolded for. Simply take him outside to allow him to fully relieve himself, and then clean up the crate. If it is not yet morning, put him back in the crate and return to bed.

Within a very short time, usually just a few days, the pup will have adjusted to this routine. As the dog ages, you will find that he can go longer and longer without having to go outside during the night. I normally add an hour for every week of age beyond the age of eight weeks. So by the time the pup is ten or eleven weeks old, he is sleeping through the night.

Leaving the Pup Behind

The time will come when you have to leave the pup in his crate at home alone. If you have taken the time to follow this introduction to crate training and have a mentally sound pup, you will probably find that this transition goes fairly smoothly. There are some steps that you should take, though, to help the process along. As with the nighttime routine, make sure that the pup has had plenty of opportunity to relieve himself before being placed in his kennel and that his water was picked up about an hour beforehand. Make his first few stints alone short periods of only two or three hours. If you have to go to work and will be gone for the entire day, try to have a neighbor or friend stop by to let the puppy out for a potty break, a bit of a drink, and some exercise. While the pup should be allowed a drink during these exercise periods, do not let him fill up too much. Do all you can to avoid having the pup soil his kennel, lest you create a situation in which this becomes the norm.

Ask your helper to stop by about every three to four hours, and be sure to go over all the steps with him. If you can't get someone to help, try making arrangements to come home at lunchtime.

You may want to let your neighbors know that you are training a new puppy, so they should not be alarmed at hearing some whining or barking for the first few days. This is normal and should be expected until the pup grows used to the routine.

One way to avoid a whining or barking pup is to be sure to give him sufficient exercise prior to crating. No one said that crate training or raising a puppy was going to be without some added commitments on your part, so you will need to adjust your routine accordingly. If you can take the time to walk the pup, play with him in the back yard, or do some training for at least twenty minutes before you crate him for an extended period, two things will likely happen. The first is that he will relieve himself before you put him in the crate, and the other is that he will tire himself out enough to settle down quickly once crated.

As discussed earlier, the crate becomes the dog's den, his sanctuary from all that goes on around him. When your dog is not being kept in his crate, leave the door open so he has ready access to it. One day, after the pup has grown older and matured a bit, you will find that he has snuck away to his kennel for a bit of rest and relaxation. You will now understand that the pup has come to fully accept his crate as his den and that you are well on your way to having a contented companion.

To have a reliable hunting spaniel, you must keep
your focus and follow a training plan.

Chapter

4

Training: An Overview

To successfully train a dog for any type of work, you must develop an action plan that will give you a fixed course along which to travel. It is rarely a quick trip from start to finish, especially if you want to be successful, but do not be daunted by the task or the length of time to reach success. If you keep your focus on the culmination of the process—a highly prized and highly praised dog—you will probably see this time go by all too quickly. So when training a spaniel to work in a controlled manner, do not allow yourself to be constrained by artificial deadlines. That way you are likely to meet with success and end up with a well-trained gundog.

It will also take some financial outlay to meet your goal. This will involve an investment in items such as training equipment and birds, fees charged by training groups or professionals, and other things that might pop up from time to time. These costs are unavoidable if you are going to develop your spaniel into a good working gundog, so prepare yourself for them. No, it will not cost you thousands and

A Clumber Spaniel at a field event. Training your dog to high levels of performance in competition or as your hunting partner requires your devotion to his training.

cated upon reasonable and agreeable goals, start by determining what your expectations or hoped-for results are.

Do you simply want a dog that will come when you call him, find birds when you need him to, and retrieve shot birds to hand? Or will you seek a dog that sits when a bird is flushed and does not give chase no matter what happens, that vigorously quarters a field with stealth and poise while remaining under the total control of his handler, and that hurls himself into the water with abandon to retrieve a bird gently to hand? Obtaining a dog like the latter one will take greater commitment than that needed to develop the other kind of dog. With an understanding that success is met by accepting your commitments and establishing an end goal to which you will dedicate yourself, you are ready to begin the process of training your dog.

Devoting Your Time

It should go without saying that the more time you spend training your dog, the faster you will reach your end goal. Proceed cautiously with the amount of time you dedicate to training each day and with the number of days you train throughout the week. Although there will be specific skills you want to instill that require

thousands of dollars to train your brush-busting, water-diving little bird-getter into a hunt'n machine, but do be prepared to spend some money to get the job done right.

What is most important for you to realize is that you must make a commitment of time if you are going to develop your dog into a well-controlled hunting companion. As with many of life's successes, it can safely be said that the dedication you show to this project will greatly determine the level to which you will be able to train your spaniel. Because dedication is often predi-

daily training activity, I generally recommend that no more than five days a week be devoted to training the dog and no more than two training periods be conducted in any one day. As a minimum, though, you need to be working with your dog at least three days a week with no more than two days of rest between training days.

Finding a happy medium is going to be relatively easy once you begin the process. Obviously, too little training is not going to get the job done. In this case, more is better, but I believe excessive training for the average individual will also impede your progress. This risk is centered on the burnout factor, which can affect both the dog and the owner. First, in considering the dog, too much training always presents you with the possibility of boring the dog and thereby breaking down his enthusiasm. A lack of enthusiasm actually makes it more difficult for the dog to retain what he learns and thereby slows down the training process, delaying success. To avoid this, employ the common rule of thumb: always leave the dog wanting more. This tends to fire up the dog for each subsequent training session and speeds the process along in a more consistent manner.

The dog is not the only one who can become burned out on training. It can be both mentally and physically strenuous for the average person who is trying to learn at the same time he is teaching. Yes, it gets better, and yes, it gets to be a whole lot of fun, but it would be irresponsible to presume that you, the trainer, will not face some stressful times yourself. Too much stress takes the trainer away from that realm of relaxation found in leisure time. If you worry more about getting in enough training time and less about the quality of the time spent, you will soon give up on the process. Keeping your training sessions limited in scope and number, especially in the first few weeks of training, may serve you and the dog better than attempting to cram more training sessions into your week or day.

As a trainer who takes his time with the process and does not push a dog further or faster than either his time or the dog's attitude seems to call for, I try to look realistically at the speed of progress. There are many trainers who will tell you, "It should not take more than ____ weeks to train a dog to ____." (You fill in the blanks.) But in my estimation, such trainers are not looking realistically at either the process or life's circumstances.

When it comes time to establish your training program, do not allow others to set unreasonable and artificial time schedules for you. Take the process at a pace that is right for you and your dog. If setbacks happen, and they will, simply accept them and continue moving along. Remember, all that matters is that you are happy with the results of your training and that your relationship with your dog is a solid one.

Where to Train

Now that you have an understanding of the time commitment you are going to be making to the training process, you need to consider where you will be doing all of this training. Most likely you are living in an urban or suburban environment and cannot simply walk out your back door and start training—or can you?

Actually, that is precisely where you will be starting your more formal work with the dog. The back yard can serve as a great place to work on everything from basic obedience to simple retrieves and more complex handling drills. Of course, you will eventually want to find more open spaces for training complex drills and introducing your pup to things such as birds and gunshots, but most of the basic or beginning work can

easily be done in the confines and comfort of your own yard.

When I first started working with spaniels, I lived in a small subdivision, and my back yard butted up against a number of my neighbors' properties. Nearly every night I was outside putting a dog or two through one drill or another, and quite frequently those drills involved the use of a training whistle. Observing my work with the dogs and seeing how the dogs were progressing became somewhat of a pastime for some of the neighbors who could easily see the goings-on. Once they heard the first whistle blast, out they came, armed with a cool beverage and a quick critique when necessary. At first their observations bothered me, but they soon became something that I was quite comfortable with and provided a bit of incentive for me to do well.

Unfortunately, the back yard will not be enough of an area for you to train your little spaniel into a finished gundog. As stated earlier, you will need some open spaces where you can allow your dog to work farther away from you and introduce him to things such as quartering, long marked retrieves, blind retrieves, and gunshots, as well as numerous other elements that make a spaniel into a hunting dog. Eventually, you will need to move your training sessions to the countryside, where releasing birds or firing off gunshots is less likely to upset the locals or bring the police roaring to your location with sirens blaring. If you are lucky, you may find some areas within your urban or suburban setting that provide you with more open space in which some drills can be run and skills instilled in your little companion.

At one time, I lived in the city and was about a mile's drive from a local community college. The college had three or four large buildings on about sixty acres of land. The majority of the acreage was actually an open commons area devoid of asphalt, concrete, roadways, and the like. It was a perfect place for my wife and me to take a couple of dogs and do some training. I taught four spaniels how to quarter a field on those grounds. I introduced them to specific whistle commands, long marked retrieves, blind retrieves, and hand signals while spending a relaxing evening on campus. Back then, I was even able to use a starter pistol to introduce them to gunshots. Today, I am not sure I could get away with such an activity. Although you may not have a cooperative college campus nearby, you may find a park here, a campus there, or some other expanse of

open ground to run your dog freely and work on some of the more extensive training drills. One training partner of mine used to train on the fairways of a bankrupt golf course, and another taught his dog some retrieving skills in a local parking garage. If you have a desire to work with your dog, you will find a means to get the job done, whether you live in town or somewhere outside it.

The rural dweller certainly does have an advantage when it comes to finding wide-open spaces. Open fields often abound in such communities, and even if you do not live on forty acres of nice grassy fields, you probably have a neighbor or two

You can start in the back yard for basic commands but will need to progress to open spaces for more advanced spaniel training.

Varying your training locations gives you access to different types of terrain and cover.

who does. A polite request and an offer of some form of compensation for allowing you to occasionally train your dog there will often be met with a willingness to do so. Of course, the urban trainer who happens to frequent a local rural community can request access to open land for training purposes. After all, the landowner probably cares less about where a person lives and more about the activity he wants to conduct and the compensation he is willing to provide.

If you are shy about asking for such permission or simply don't believe in bothering someone with this type of request, you may find that your state government has public areas set aside for gundog training. Open to the public, these areas allow you to freely run your dog, fire off gunshots, and occasionally release birds for the purpose of training. Such locations are usually highly regulated, so you should contact your Natural Resources or Game and Fish Department to see if such facilities are available in your area and to acquaint yourself with the regulations regarding dog training.

Many areas of the country have spaniel field training clubs that provide both grounds and training assistance to their members and guests. Every new puppy buyer should find out whether such a group exists in his area and, if it does, speak with the group about joining. These groups are often a godsend for the spaniel trainer, as they can provide help in so many ways. Although it is not impossible to train a spaniel by yourself, it sure is a lot easier when you have others willing to help. A group like this usually has experienced members to provide training critiques, insight, and assistance to everyone. It also has access to birds, which are both an essential part of the training equation and sometimes difficult to obtain, let alone house. Finding the local spaniel training club will be one of the best things you can do to help ensure a successful outcome with your hunting spaniel.

Although training groups are good and well worth your participation, look also for professional trainers within a reasonable drive of your home. Many professionals have a mixed bag of services available; these often include hourly rates for the person who simply wants some occasional help in getting over a hurdle or solving a problem. Some trainers will also rent you the use of their training fields and even sell you birds when you need them. The key here is to be willing to put forth a little extra cash for the benefit of any of these services; they are all well worth the money spent.

Finally, if you are looking for some training grounds and a source for birds, check with the local game preserves. Often these facilities will allow their members to use the grounds for dog training in the off-season. Some even have experienced trainers who can help you when problems or questions arise in your training program.

Finding a location or two in which to train is not an easy task, but it is an essential one, and you now have an idea of where to start looking. Once you find a location, keep searching for more, because having multiple spots for field training will be a bonus to you and the dog. Such variety prevents the

dog from becoming so accustomed to a particular location that he knows what to expect before you even begin your work, and it keeps you from wearing out your welcome at any one site. In my area, I train with three different groups and on four different field grounds. My dogs never know what to expect at any one place, and sometimes neither do I.

All About Birds

"You can't train a bird dog without birds!" That would seem to go without saying, but what kind of birds should you use, and where will you find them?

Because they are easy to use, pigeons are usually the birds of choice when introducing birds in training.

Later in your dog's training and in actual fieldwork, he will be able to retrieve larger birds.

In the good ol' days, many dogs were trained on the job. They got their instruction by hitting the fields on a regular basis throughout the hunting season and, if lucky, during the off-season as well. These dogs cut their teeth on the ways of the crafty pheasant born and raised in the wild. Such birds learned quickly that their lives depended on avoiding predators of all types, and they used their instinctive skills to outwit many a gundog. If a dog was going to be worth his keep, he would have to learn how to outsmart those birds and produce them for the guns. Thus, most dogs did not learn these things through rote drills or through fancy training techniques but by sheer trial and error.

Were these dogs somehow smarter or better than the gundogs of today? Some hunters would argue yes, but most others would claim no. I straddle the fence on this issue, believing that there is nothing better than an experienced gundog raised on wild birds but recognizing that in today's society fewer dogs have the opportunity to gain such experience, and so other means must be employed. I also recognize that while the dogs of grandpa's and great-grandpa's day may have been well versed in the ways of wild birds, outside of the field-trial game few were as well controlled and responsive to their owners as today's dogs trained on pen-raised birds and systematically drilled on specific skills. What is true in all cases is that you will never make a spaniel into a solid gundog without the use of birds, so let's consider the options available to you.

MOST COMMONLY USED BIRDS
There are three birds commonly used for spaniel training and a few others that can be used in a pinch. Most common is the pigeon, followed by the chukar, and finally the pheasant. Others that can be employed are the larger variety of

quail and Hungarian partridge. All of these birds, even the commonly used species, have their drawbacks at times, and some states require a special permit to use any of them for dog training. Always check with your state agencies to be sure that you meet all of the regulations.

Because of their relatively low cost, ease of care, hardiness, and reasonable flight qualities, pigeons are probably used more often than any other species. Obtaining them is not as easy as it once was, but at the right time of the year and in the right location, they can be bought for a few dollars each. Compare that cost with the cost of pheasants, which can run as much as ten dollars per bird, and you can see that you might get more bang for your buck with pigeons. Those who have the space to keep a small colony of pigeons in a coop (something often done in the city as well as outside of it) will also find that these birds are cheaper to feed and house than pheasants are and can even be trained to return to the coop should they be released, thus rendering themselves reusable, which can come in quite handy at times.

Another excellent quality of the pigeon is that once it is put down in the field, it will often stay put as opposed to running off before the handler can get his dog to the area.

This means that there is going to be a bird where the handler expects one, and it allows the trainer to be prepared to reinforce whatever behavior is being instilled at the time. Furthermore, the pigeon's small size makes it an ideal bird for young dogs or the smaller spaniel breeds. Since most states consider pigeons to be a nongame species, it is normally legal to train dogs with pigeons throughout the year. All in all, it is an ideal training bird.

Another bird of similar size but having stronger flight capability and a tendency to run is the chukar. This is a rather hardy bird as well, and it,

With a puppy, you want to use small birds that he can easily manage.

too, can be reused for training purposes in many circumstances. These birds tend to consume a bit more food and do not return to the coop as readily as pigeons do, but they will covey up and seek others of their kind in a manner similar to that of quail. This tendency has allowed me to recapture some of my training birds and save more than a few dollars in bird costs. At roughly two to three times the cost of pigeons, chukar are not your cheapest training birds, but they make darned good ones. If I have one complaint about the chukar, it is that it will often run if not placed in the field properly. Although this can be a great training opportunity—tracking a running chukar helps a dog learn the art of trailing—it can also change your game plan when the bird you thought would be busting out of cover has run off, and your dog is left without a bird to flush. Chukar can be found at many of the game preserves, and many states have game bird breeders who raise chukar and will sell them in small quantities. As with the pigeon, most states do not classify chukar as a game species, and they will allow you to train with them throughout the year.

For many reasons pheasants do not make the best training bird, but if you are going to hunt them or run your dog in field trials or hunt tests one day, you had better train with them. Their cost, even when purchased in a large quantity, is too prohibitive to make them economical, and their size makes them harder to keep on hand or be used with a young dog. The aggressiveness of a crippled rooster pheasant that is pecking and spurring a young dog as he tries to retrieve the bird to his handler has been known to produce training setbacks that are very difficult to overcome. Because of this, pheasants should always be used on dogs that are further along in their training and have matured to a point where such intimidation will not adversely affect them. Like the chukar, pheasants have a tendency to get up and run rather than fly off when they sense danger approaching, and they will often not fly from cover unless they feel there is no other option, so expect to give your dog some added training on trailing scent when you use pheasants.

I do not usually begin using pheasants in my training scheme until the latter part of the training season, which in my area begins to wind down in September. By the time August comes around, I like to have pheasants available to me so that I can get the dog a bit more used to both the scent and the feel of these birds prior to the start of hunting season. This is another reason for having access to a game preserve, where you can work your dog and have a supply of pheasants available.

If you are running your dog in hunt tests or field trials during the year, you will more often than not get plenty of work on pheasants. The pheasant and the chukar are the birds of choice for most of these events, and your dog needs to be familiar with them if he is going to get through such events success-fully.

As mentioned earlier, there are other birds that can be used for training, but they are not as ideal or as appropriate as the pigeon, chukar, or pheasant. The larger varieties of quail will work in a pinch for young dogs that simply need to get their noses into birds, make some simple retrieves, and so forth. Because these birds do not hold well when planted and tend to covey up with others of their species, they present challenges that do not make training go very easily or very well at times. The same is true, although to a lesser extent, for the Hungarian partridge. These birds are a bit larger than quail but also have the tendency to move too much once put down in the field.

Additionally, both of these birds are considered game birds in a number of states, so their use will be more restricted.

HOW TO USE BIRDS

How the birds are used is primarily determined by your objective. A young dog, just starting to learn how to quarter a field, for instance, may have a bird "thrown into" light cover and not really "planted" *per se*. The advanced dog, needing to be tested on his abilities, will likely have a number of birds that are planted along a predetermined course in a variety of cover condi-tions to more closely simulate a real hunting situation.

A gentle grip, also known as a *soft mouth*, is preferred by all gundog enthusiasts.

How you go about planting birds will vary by the type of bird you are working with, the cover you are working in, and sometimes even the weather. If you are working with a local training group, you will find that there are probably a couple of members who have become quite skilled at planting birds. Make friends with these people, and learn their skills as best you can. Good bird planting often leads to more successful dog training.

As with almost everything we do, bird handling requires that you have a few special supplies on hand. First of all, you will need a bird box for transporting your birds to the field, and you should have some feed and water available for them if you will be housing them overnight or for a few days prior to use. Gloves are essential for maintaining a good hold on a bird and avoiding any contamination. Birds, especially pen-raised birds, are not the cleanest animals and can carry a number of nasty little bugs, so wear gloves when handling them. A "bird bag" (a mesh bag used for carrying live birds in the field) is a handy item and will give you the ability to carry birds easily and safely while working with your dog. Duct tape, that universally essential tool, can be employed to restrict the use of one wing, which prevents a bird from

flying off. Finally, on hot and sunny days you need to have a tarp or other covering that can provide the birds with some shade so they do not become overheated. The tarp will also come in handy to keep the birds from getting too wet when a light rain is falling.

Birds are mostly used in one of two ways. Either they are used as a teaser to help instill drive or they are used to simulate a true-to-life experience. The teasers are often "taped-wing" birds that have had one wing taped so that they are thrown off balance and are either unable to fly at all or for no more than a short distance. It does not take a great deal of tape to accomplish this. A piece of tape about one inch wide and long enough to wrap around the wing and bind some of the primary feathers should do the trick. Duct tape is the best to use as it bonds well and will not come free, which would allow the bird to fly off. All of the different birds can have their wings taped with no adverse affects to the bird, other than possibly losing a few feathers.

Before you start training your dog in any particular area, take the time to lay out your course, giving strong consideration to wind dir-ection, terrain, and the amount of cover you have available. Do not forget to look the field over for ideal planting locations. Watch for pockets of open areas where it may be difficult to plant a bird and where your dog may have to cover a lot of empty ground before coming upon a bird. For the more experienced dog, this may not be a bad thing, but if you want to get your dog's nose into birds in rapid succession, you will have difficulty doing so if there are too many areas devoid of sufficient cover.

As you walk and inspect the field prior to starting, you may wish to mark the locations for planting with small pieces of surveyor's tape. Make sure that this is subtle enough that the dog does not notice the tape. Marking planting areas saves you time by helping you remember where you plan to put your birds or where you placed them earlier.

When laying out a training course, pick a start point and an end point that are maybe 100 yards apart. Draw an imaginary line between these two points (called the center line); when you plant the birds, begin on one side of the line, then plant the next bird on the opposite side. The distance between the birds, how far you plant from the center line, and the number of birds you plant will vary based upon what you are trying to accomplish that day. (There will be more on that in later chapters.)

The type of cover you are dealing with has a lot to do with how you are going to plant the birds. If they go into very thick cover, you will have your dog trapping or catching the birds before they ever get off the ground. In cover that is too light, they will run or fly off before you get the chance to have your dog hit the field, and it soon becomes quite depressing to watch a $5 to $10 bill flying off to places unknown. Unfortunately, the

This is a good example of moderate cover that allows the handler to easily see the dog yet is heavy enough that the birds will stay in position.

best way for you to learn what cover is ideal is by trial and error. Sure, you can get a good idea by watching others do the planting, but only when you have laid down a few birds yourself will you begin to get a real feel for the proper conditions for planting birds.

When it comes to planting pigeons, the common method is the shake and toss. Grasp the bird in one hand, with the bird's wings held firmly against its body. Hold the bird upside down so that its head is pointed toward the ground, and shake the bird back and forth in an effort to make it dizzy. This can take a bit of time; don't rush it, and don't be too vigorous with your shaking. You have heard of shaken baby syndrome? Well, you can have shaken bird syndrome, too, so remember you are trying to only dizzy the bird, not render it unconscious. After giving the bird a good shake, firmly toss it into light cover. A pigeon thrown into heavy cover with no clear exit will likely be trapped by the dog. When tossing the bird into cover, be sure to toss at a downward angle as opposed to lobbing it out in front of you. If you throw the bird out and away, it will likely simply recover and fly off before it ever hits the ground.

Pigeons cannot launch themselves the way pheasants or chukar can. They need a clearer opening to become airborne, so the amount of cover matters with these guys. Too little cover and the bird will be on its way; too much cover and your little brush-buster will snatch the bird up before it knows what happened. I find that a firm toss of the pigeon usually guarantees that the bird will stay on the ground when it is thrown into cover, especially if it is not quite dizzy. A gentle toss often seems to give the bird the opportunity to get airborne and fly away, which we don't want.

Chukar are probably the easiest of all birds to plant. Although some people like to plant them just as they do pigeons (a technique that usually results in a heavier plant), I find that the best way is to simply hold the bird upside down by its feet while carrying it to the location of the plant. Then I gently swing the bird back and forth (as though my arm were a swing) for a minute or so before dropping it into place. This may produce a light plant, meaning that the bird may get up and move a bit more than with a heavy plant. To avoid that problem, hold the bird upside down longer and swing it more before dropping it in place. One nice thing about chukar is that they will often burrow into the cover a bit and stay put. If you put them in light cover, however, and they see an escape route, they will be off like little roadrunners, so moderate cover is best for these guys.

In addition, if you use the same technique as was described above for planting pigeons, you need to understand that the chukar is a much stronger and more agile bird. Tossing them often leads to fly-aways, which then lead to trapped birds as you try to compensate for the problem by putting the birds down even harder.

The pheasant is the most difficult of all birds to plant. Their size and strength make it hard to nearly impossible to use either of the methods discussed earlier, although you can sometimes be successful with these techniques when planting hen pheasants. One problem with hens is found in the spring, when they are producing eggs. Egg-laden birds will often hold tight when planted but have difficulty flying; therefore, I try to avoid springtime hen pheasants. Roosters, on the other hand, are a good bet at any time of the year. If you don't have moderate to heavy cover, though, you should avoid using pheasants for training. Without such cover, they will recuperate from whatever planting method you use and either run or fly away.

There are two primary methods for planting pheasants. The first is the same as the pigeon method except that, because of the pheasants' size, you will want to use two hands while dizzying the birds, and you are better off placing them in the cover rather than throwing them in. The second method involves "sleeping" the bird, which can be done in various ways to relax a bird in cover. The simplest is to get a firm grip on the bird, usually with one hand holding the feet or legs still, and then tuck its head under one wing, holding the wing firmly against the body until the bird begins to relax a bit. Then set the bird in cover and slowly release your hands as you move away quickly, trying not to disturb the bird. A third method uses much the same technique but has you gently stretching the bird's legs outward, toward the end of its tail. After a short time, you will see the bird begin to relax. Place the bird in cover belly up and pull a little extra grass or other cover material over it before walking away. Once you get the hang of it, any of these methods will normally result in a bird that stays put and flushes well as long as you have plenty of cover.

LIVE BIRDS/DEAD BIRDS

Before we leave the topic of birds and bird planting, let's take a minute to talk about the reality of

The breeder introduces a curious litter of pups to bird wings.

your training sessions. If you want to train a flushing dog to the peak of performance, or even to a mediocre level for that matter, you will need to work with live birds on a fairly frequent basis. But what if you don't have good access to birds? What if you don't have the time to drive from suburbia to the countryside three or four nights a week? What happens then? Is there something you can do to keep the skill set expanding and to keep your dog's nose in birds?

In a word, yes. Even the most inexperienced trainer is probably familiar with the concept of using bird wings in puppy or fundamental training sessions. The wings, having been detached from dead game birds or pigeons, are stored in your freezer and attached to retrieving bumpers with duct tape, rubber bands, or Velcro straps to allow you to introduce the dog to bird scent and the feel of feathers. If you do not have ready access to game bird wings, try contacting your local game farm and asking them for a supply. They should be happy to give you all you need. If you still can't find a supply, then check out the various dog-training supply houses, as many of them now sell wings. Using bird wings is a simple way to keep the bird element in your training process, but it loses its edge as the dog matures and expands his abilities.

As the dog grows older and wiser, he will benefit from the use of dead birds in training when live birds are unavailable. I suggest that you try to keep a ready supply of dead frozen birds in your freezer, including pigeons or chukar, a few pheasants, and a small supply of ducks (best for water retrieves). Frozen birds come in handy for everything from fixing retrieving problems to establishing a quartering pattern to setting up water retrieves.

In general, allow the birds to thaw for about two to four hours prior to use. This will make them feel less like frozen rocks and more like firm birds. A dog that has a gentle pickup and delivery (retrieve) will not do much harm to these frozen birds, and you will be able to use them over and over again. It is not unusual to get several training sessions out of a single bird. We will discuss in later chapters some of the methods involved with frozen birds.

Training Stages

Before we progress much further, here is what you should expect from the following pages and chapters. I have broken the training down into five stages: laying a foundation (this chapter), the fundamentals (chapter 5), the started dog (chapter 6), moving on up (chapter 7), and advanced training (chapter 8). Each stage will have a specific set of goals to accomplish, and your success at one step is dependent upon your success at the previous step. I have tried to incorporate into each chapter work that can be done at home (yard work), some overviews of the equipment needed and how to use it, general goals that you should attempt to accomplish, and discussions about where you might run into trouble. One point I would like to make here is that whenever you find yourself running into trouble,

take a step back and try to analyze the reason you have hit this snag. Often the reason will be found by looking in the mirror, for it will have been your failure to instill the basic understanding that your dog needs before he can move on to more advanced work.

Every trainer, amateur and pro, stumbles from time to time. The better trainers, those who don't give up when they stumble, have two things going for them: the ability to recognize the core problem and the willingness to take a step back to overcome that problem. I often tell people that the best way to overcome a problem is to break the problem down to its individual elements and rebuild from there.

The scent and feel of a bird wing rouse a pup's natural hunting instincts.

For instance, let's say that your dog likes to pick up the bird and run around with it a bit before bringing it to you. Most inexperienced and even a few experienced people would say that the dog has a poor retrieve or "likes to show off his prize," which is simply an excuse for not wanting or knowing how to correct the behavior. When I tell them that the dog has a problem not with retrieving—after all, he eventually brings the bird to the trainer—but with his recall or his *come* command, they are often surprised. But that is exactly where the problem lies.

Let me give you some insight into what I am saying. A retrieve consists of four principal steps: go to the bird, pick up the bird, go to the trainer, give the bird to the trainer. The dog that parades around with the bird in his mouth before taking it to the handler has completed the first two steps of the retrieve just fine; he has gotten to the bird and picked it up. What he has not done is return it to the trainer quickly enough. This is the point at which the breakdown has occurred, and as returning to the handler is a simple come command, that is the element that must be worked on. So when I tell a trainer that his dog's poor retrieve is based upon a poor "come" and that he

should work on the come command more and the retrieve less, it is because the dog has learned that there are times when he does not need to come right away—like when he has a bird in his mouth. What the trainer needs to do to fix such a problem is to concentrate on obedience exercises that teach the dog to come every single time without delay. Once the dog is coming well, the "retrieve problem" usually disappears in short order.

Stumbling in training is one thing, but roadblocks are another matter. When you come to a point in training at which you simply cannot get beyond a hurdle or have exhausted all avenues and you need help—ask. Ask your friends in the local training club you have joined. Ask the local pro you visit with from time to time. Ask the successful participant you watch during a hunt test. Ask and you will gain insight into your problem and continue on a path to success. Keep silent and you will get nowhere.

Although I have tried to include some of the more common setbacks in training within each of the following sections, many others exist and will undoubtedly raise their ugly heads. With the minor exception of two or three problems, most are overcome with insight, time, and dedication by even the most inexperienced trainer. So roll up your sleeves, and let's get started on turning that cute little pup into a top-notch gundog.

Laying the Foundation

There was a time when children began their education with no preparation at all, no day care and no preschool. When a child left his mother's side and walked into the classroom for the first time, it was a whole new world, with little warning of what to expect and no preparation for what was to unfold over the next dozen or more years. Today, a child who enters school without some form of preschool education often is seen as missing the fundamentals needed to start a lifetime of learning.

Like children, gundogs once began their education with little exposure to the fundamentals. Except in the most knowledgeable of homes or training kennels, few dogs had much preparation for "learning to learn" and were simply plopped down in a field one day to begin their education. Today, things are different.

Whether this change correlates to the evolution of our educational system or simply happens to exist because of an improvement in our understanding of canine behavior and learning, we have come a long way from the days of old. Today, we have a bevy of established and proven training programs at our disposal, and we begin training at an earlier age than ever before, or at least we should. Pick up a dog-training book or magazine article from forty or more years ago, and you are probably going to read that you should not start training your pup until he is at least six months old because he will not be mature enough to learn before then. If you were to take that approach today, you would be well behind many other trainers. In fact, today most hunt test programs are open to six-month-old dogs, and they are expected to have already mastered a particular set of skills. What is sometimes expected of a six-month-old today would not have been the norm for a dog nearly twice that age a generation ago.

When do we begin to lay the foundation? That depends upon whether we are talking about informal or formal training. Informal training can often begin within days, if not hours, of your pup's arrival; more formal training is usually not begun until that new pup has settled into his home and begun to bond with you, roughly within a week or two of his arrival at your home. Of course, like all new gundog owners, you will want to get the little guy chasing birds, fetching his bumpers, and enduring gunshots a few hours after his arrival, but I hope you will be smart enough to know better. There is no need to rush. Like every good builder, you need to lay a solid foundation before you begin to raise your structure. In gundog training, that foundation starts with socialization, generally accepted good manners, and basic obedience training, all of which you will need to begin working on soon after the dog's arrival.

Because this is a book on field training the spaniel, it will focus only on that which most directly affects your ability to achieve your end goal. Other books, seminars, videos, and local professionals are at your disposal for a more in-depth education regarding socialization, good manners, and obedience, and I urge you to utilize any of them in the process of developing your gundog. Here we will take a preliminary look at why all three areas are important elements in your dog's development.

Socialization and Manners

Socialization means many things within the dog world, but for our purposes it simply means the development of a dog that is friendly, perhaps outgoing, and willing to accept and adapt to new environments. Now most of these attributes are going to be based on the dog's genetic makeup as much as, if not more than, any type of training. For instance, the dog that is a bit aloof as a seven- or eight-week-old pup will probably remain so all his life, whereas his outgoing littermate, who jumps into everyone's lap, will probably always be the life of the party. Although socialization may not be able to completely reverse the effects of a dog's genetic tendencies (such as making a fearful dog secure in his own skin), it can help prevent those genetic leanings from being changed (such as making a secure dog fearful) by a lack of exposure. I believe that socialization classes and programs usually succeed at preventing problems from developing in most dogs, and they are vital to having a sound dog of any breed or type.

Picture yourself arriving at your training club's grounds for your first morning in the field. You climb out of your vehicle, go to your dog's travel crate, and attach a leash to his collar. The dog appears to not want to come out. You wonder why but shrug it off as you ease him from the crate. He hits the ground and immediately hugs your leg as you walk to greet the other club members. You proudly introduce your new pup, who is now a couple of steps behind you, and as your friends reach to pet your pup, he attempts to run back to your car, stopped only by the leash. You shrug it off.

A short while later, the bird boxes are unloaded and set out in the field, so you think that this is an opportunity to get your dog's nose on birds and get him excited. You walk over to one of the boxes, filled with excitement as you expect your pup to go crazy over the birds, but all he does is try to run away, tugging to get back to his crate. You shrug it off.

Then a wise and observant fellow club member comes over and says something like, "He's a bit of a fearful one, eh? You best work on that before you ever cut him loose in the field. We don't want any dogs lost out here." Your heart sinks. The excitement drains, and you feel at a loss. Why did this happen? Why would a dog that is normally so outgoing and excited act like this?

The answer is probably that the dog has not been socialized. Socialization is best started young, before your pup even arrives at your home. A good breeder does a lot to begin the socialization process, but you have a role to play as well. You need to take steps to constantly expose your dog, beginning within

Important early socialization starts within the litter as the pups play together and the breeder exposes them to new experiences.

days of his arrival to your home, to new and different situations throughout his early months and even years of life. You should take the dog to all types of events, such as the kids' baseball games, the local farmers' market, walks around the neighborhood to meet other dogs and people, the community parade on the Fourth of July, and anywhere else you can think of.

Such trips give the dog the opportunity to experience different environments in a controlled manner without a need for him to be pushed and with lots of positive rewards (such as food treats) available. With limited pressure, the ability to get a pleasant snack, and a lot of petting from children and adults, a young dog tends to grow up less fearful of things and comes to like exposure to new environments, meeting and greeting others, and new sights and sounds. In short, you need to have a well-socialized dog in order to have a well-balanced gundog in the field. Check with your veterinarian or local kennel club for references on trainers offering socialization classes for young dogs.

Have you ever walked into a friend's home and been greeted by a rambunctious dog that jumps on you and nearly knocks you over? Have you known a dog that was adept at snatching food from the countertop or table when his owner was not looking? Or how about a dog that barks at every sight and sound that is unfamiliar or that he finds exciting? If you have been around dogs for very long, the answer to these questions will undoubtedly be yes. All of these are inappropriate behaviors and simply bad manners, but thankfully all are curable, and more important, they are all preventable if the dog is given the proper upbringing. Why are such behaviors pertinent to a discussion about gundog training? Because an unmannered dog is likely one that either has not been trained at all or has not learned—through a sound training program—just what

his proper role is in his pack, your household.

An ill-mannered dog is going to be harder to train because he is going to be less willing to take direction and conform to your standards. And why should he? If he has learned that he can do as he pleases within his normal surroundings, certainly he has no reason to believe that he needs to act differently in any other environment. After all, dogs are not like people, who can differentiate between different settings and act accordingly. To avoid problem behavior in the field, establish a fixed set of behaviors that will be expected of the dog in his home environment, and be sure to uphold those expectations in all other settings as well.

Obedience: An Overview

The primary ingredient needed to build your training foundation is obedience; without it, you will not be able to bind all of the other ingredients together. The need for obedience training goes beyond the objective of developing a sound gundog and extends to other areas, such as keeping your dog safe and secure. Pay particular attention to your instruction in this area.

This training can begin within days if not hours of first getting your pup. It is imperative that the training be done in a consistent manner by all who are involved with the pup (spouse, children, nanny, visitors, and so forth). Consistency is both the cornerstone of a sound training program and a necessary tool to move the process along with few hurdles. To start, you should take the time, preferably before your dog arrives at your home, to develop a list of commands, with their meanings well defined, that will be used to control and direct your dog's behavior. You need to share this list with other family members, friends, and caretakers who may come in contact with the pup.

Although your list of commands can be as long and varied as you would like it to be, there are six key commands that I think every spaniel needs to understand. In no order of importance, these commands are *hup* (spaniel parlance for "sit"), *heel, come, down, stay,* and *no.* Other commands that can be quite useful are *kennel* and *place.* Before moving on to how to teach these different commands, here is a definition for each.

COMMAND DEFINITIONS
Hup/Sit—Spaniel enthusiasts have used the term *hup* in place of *sit* for a very long time, but it is purely a matter of tradition. If you want to use *sit* instead, go right ahead. No matter which word is used, they both mean that the dog should put his rump on the ground and keep it there.

Heel—This command tells the dog to get to your left or right side.

This Clumber Spaniel is in a sit/stay in heel position at his owner's left side.

As a hunting spaniel does much of his work off leash, a reliable *come* command is essential.

The down is a submissive position; therefore, the pup may need a little extra coaxing to perform this exercise.

It does not matter if the dog is walking with you or sitting next to you, "heel" means that he is to be at your side. Traditionally, we heel our dogs on our left side. Why? I don't think that anyone knows anymore, but one explanation I heard was that the average person is right-handed and carries his gun on his right side. Having the dog heel on the left keeps the dog out of the way of the gun. That seems as plausible an explanation as one can have. If you want to break with tradition and have your dog heel on the right, go ahead; just be consistent. Understand, too, that some of the dog games we play—obedience trials for instance—may require that you have your dog heel on the left. Finally, when it comes to field work there can be an advantage to having your dog heel on both sides. In this case you will need one command to tell a dog to heel on the left and another to tell him to heel on the right. One of the first dogs I ever trained to do this was trained to understand the traditional heel and then taught that when I said "right," she was to immediately get to my right side. She learned the difference in just three days.

Come/Here—The command that tells a dog to return to you is *come*, or in some communities, *here*. As with all commands, which one you choose is a matter of preference. I like to stick with *come*. I think that the word *come* has a firmer, more deliberate "you must comply" type of tone to it than *here* does. Since this is one of those commands that can save a dog's life, it is a command that you should stress in training and work on in all types of environments.

Down—This means to lie down and should not be confused with telling the dog to get off a person or piece of furniture; for those situations, use the word *off*. Although many field trainers say that a gundog does not need to learn the *down* command, I believe it is a valuable tool that can come in handy in the field as well as at home. This command helps instill control over the dog and puts him into a submissive position, where he must acquiesce to the trainer's wishes. That helps the dog understand his proper role in the household, or his pack, and that will go a long way toward getting cooperation in the future.

Stay—If you want your dog to remain where he is without moving, then use the command *stay*. If your dog is sitting and you tell him to stay, he should remain sitting and remain where he is when you give the command. That seems self-evident, but many people seem to believe that a dog that creeps from one spot or the other without moving too far is still staying. This is simply not the case. The old adage "Give him an inch and he will take a mile" really applies here. If you do not insist on the full meaning of stay, you will end up with a dog that is never going to be truly steady to wing and shot or steady at the line when working as a retriever. If you want a dog that will not bolt out the door when you go to get the morning paper, not leap from the truck unexpectedly when you are getting ready to head to the field, or not chase after that bird you just missed, concentrate on instilling this command.

No—Yes, *no* is a command. It means "stop"—stop doing whatever. For example, if the dog is barking, we tell him "no," meaning "stop barking." If he is digging in the rose garden, we tell him "no," meaning "stop your digging." All commands are learned through a series of frequent repetition, perhaps none more so than "no."

Kennel—It is hoped that, starting in early puppyhood, you will raise your dog to be housed in a dog crate when he cannot be watched. This process is often referred to as crate training and was discussed in chapter 3. If you read that chapter, you already know that "kennel" is the command used to tell a dog to go to his kennel or crate. If you haven't read the chapter, then now might be a good time to do so.

Place—This is a very useful and sometimes overlooked command that is more often used in retriever or obedience circles than with field training spaniels. However, if you are going to use your dog as a nonslip retriever or if you want a well-controlled house dog, then this is a command to teach your dog. The *place* command really means "go to" as in "go to your rug and stay there until I release you." When the dog is in his place, he is free to move around and relax, but he must not leave the established spot. Some people confuse *place* with *stay*, but when a dog is told to stay, he must not move. We'll talk about this a bit more later, but remember that there is a definite difference between the two commands.

The aforementioned are the foundation commands. You and the dog will be learning a number of other commands as we move along, but for now these are it. Well, almost. Before you actually begin to train the dog, you need to establish a release word. What is a release word? It is the word used to tell the dog that he is free to go about his business and is no longer under command. Generally speaking, until the dog is released, he should be following whatever command he was last given. If he was last told to sit, he should be sitting. If he was last told to stay, he should still be where you told him to stay. The common release words are *OK* and *free*. Pick one and stick with it. I prefer *free* because it is less commonly used in our everyday expressions than is *OK*. Either will work just fine, though; simply be consistent in your application.

COMMAND TONES

The tone used when giving a command is almost as important as the consistency with which a command is applied. Generally, commands should be given in a clear and concise manner, providing little inflection to the voice and coming across as matter-of-fact. Adding inflection can create problems as the dog begins to differentiate between the differing tones used.

For example, let's say that you command your dog to sit simply by saying, "Rover, sit." Now let's say that when Rover doesn't sit, you add a little pleading to your tone, as in, "Roooverr, siiiiit?" And finally, after a few more such requests, you give up and bellow out "ROVER, SIT!!!!" as you march over to him and push his little behind to the floor. Well, what do you think that Rover is learning? Actually, he is learning a number of things, but primarily he is learning that he doesn't really have to sit until he hears the right tone, which is "ROVER, SIT!!!!" Now it is impractical to expect you or any other human being to never yell at or plead with your dog, but try your best not to. Keeping the command tones consistent and matter-of-fact will help you avoid confusing the dog and will speed up training.

Notice, too, that my examples indicate for you to give the dog's name first and then the command. There is a bit of disagreement on this among many trainers, but I firmly believe that using the name is necessary. This is especially true if there are others besides just you and the dog living in the house or when you are out and about the marshes, meadows, and world in general. Giving the dog's name first allows you to both get his attention and let him know that you are talking to him and no one else.

DOGS CAN COUNT

I remember watching television years ago and seeing a horse that could count. Its handler would ask it a question that required a numerical answer, and sure enough the horse would pound its hoof to the ground the correct number of times to indicate the answer. Of course, the horse was not really counting, but it gave the impression that it was, which provided for a nice piece of entertainment. Well, dogs have the ability to perform a little calculation themselves if their training is not applied in the correct manner.

When first training a pup to respond to a command, the training sequence follows a set format, in which the command is given as the dog performs the command, and the dog is then rewarded for his behavior. Over time, the pup associates the command word with the action and performs the action on cue with no or little need for a reward. Once the pup has an understanding of the command and what is expected, failure to comply brings some form of reprimand, and it is at this point that the dog will learn to count. If the trainer does not insist on compliance after just one iteration of the command but waits for, say, three attempts before requiring compliance, the dog will soon learn that he does not have to comply until he is told that third time. In essence, he learns to count to three. To prevent your dog from learning to count, insist upon swift and determined compliance to a known command the first time you give it.

A firm foundation in basic obedience lays the
groundwork for success in fieldwork.

Teaching the Fundamentals

With the basic nuances of the training process outlined, it is time to move on to the fundamentals. These include areas specific to the hunting spaniel as well as basic obedience and will help you form a solid foundation for your training program.

Obedience, Leash Breaking, and Corrections

OBEDIENCE

You can begin very basic obedience training soon after your pup arrives, but it is best if you wait until he understands his name, which should take just a few short days. Initial training is likely to take place indoors as you teach your pup such things as "sit" and "come" while lounging around the house. I refer to this as informal training because you are not setting aside a specific block of time to train; rather, you are taking advantage of situations around the house that allow you to instill simple commands in the dog. When you do decide to begin your obedience training, you will need to set aside two or three periods each day where you will do little else but train the dog on his commands. The sessions should last for fifteen to twenty minutes each and take place in different locations.

I like to start all obedience training with the use of food as both a reward and a lure. Because puppies have usually not yet developed a discerning palate, the easiest type of treat to use is a piece of the pup's kibble. Most pups will react as positively to that as they will to a small piece of hot dog or dried liver, and kibble is a lot less messy to use. Keeping a couple of small dishes of kibble scattered around the home but out of reach of the pup assures that a reward is close at hand and increases the opportunities you will have to train. Eventually, you will wean yourself and the pup off food rewards and move on to other reward structures, but plan to use food for the better part of his obedience training program.

Although most dogs are trained by just one person in the household, it will not hurt a bit for you to have your partner and children involved from time to time as well. As a companion animal, the pup has to understand that he potentially has numerous leaders, and one of the best ways for that to happen is for those other leaders to participate in some of the training. Additionally, having others work with the pup assures that everyone is on the same page when it comes to commands and expectations. Observe your training assistants as they work with the dog, and make certain that what

Training Tools

When it comes to establishing the training fundamentals, you need only a handful of tools, consisting of the following:
- Collars: a flat buckle collar and a metal slip (choke) collar.
- A variety of leashes in a variety of lengths: 6-foot leather leash, 20-foot long line, and 25-foot flexible leash.
- A bait bag, which is a handy little item that normally attaches to your belt and is used to hold food treats during your training session.
- Two whistles and a double lanyard to hold both: a spaniel whistle and a retriever whistle.
- A canvas puppy bumper.
- A training pistol capable of firing shotgun primers.

they are doing corresponds to your approach.

As was mentioned earlier, you want to have a variety of locations where you train your pup. This is true of both obedience and field training, and for good reason. Dogs are very place-conscious and come to attribute a specific set of behaviors to a specific place. By mixing up the training locations, the dog comes to understand that compliance is necessary no matter where he happens to be when a command is given. Another advantage obtained by changing locations is having the dog exposed to different sights, sounds, and smells that distract him from the task at hand. The greater the variety, the better controlled your dog will be over time. However, do not rush into new surroundings until you are certain your dog has a solid understanding of what you are teaching, or you will risk delaying your progress.

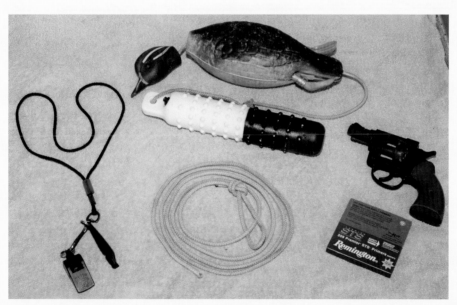

A few of the simple tools used for training your dog in the field include the following (CLOCKWISE FROM TOP): retrieving bumpers, a training pistol that shoots shotgun primers, a belt cord, and two types of whistles (retriever whistle on the left and spaniel whistle on the right).

Necessary training tools are a leash and a metal slip, or choke, collar.

When it comes to formal training, I try to minimize distractions by training in a relatively roomy indoor space, such as the basement or an empty garage, and I banish all other people and animals from that area. I want the dog's concentration to be on me rather than on what might be going on around us. This is not the time to be in the back yard on a blustery day with leaves blowing around, songbirds flying by, and the neighbor's children playing next door. Although you would eventually get the pup trained in such surroundings, the pace of learning would be slow and your level of frustration quite high. Exposure to distractions should come only after a good basic understanding has been reached.

I believe that all formal obedience training should involve the use of a 1/2-inch-wide, 6-foot-long leather leash and a chain slip collar, also known as a choke collar (a terrible misnomer). A leather leash has just the right feel; it is not too flimsy or too stiff and will hold up to years of use. Do not get a braided leather leash because, although quite elegant-looking, it can inflict a pretty good burn on your hand if the dog decides to bolt and catches you unaware; the same is true of nylon leashes.

To hold the leash properly, place the loop end in your right hand (assuming the dog will be heeling on your left), and reach your left hand over the top of the leash as you take hold of it. Your left hand should hold the leash so that when your hand is hanging comfortably at your side, you are neither tugging on the collar nor giving so much slack that the pup can wander far from your side.

The slip collar is made up of a length of metal chain with two metal "O" rings attached to each end. To assemble such a collar, feed the chain through one ring, bringing the two rings together. A slip collar, when properly used, will provide the right form of control and correction needed to reinforce commands. A slip collar should be used only when there may be a need to control the dog on leash, and this type of collar should never be left on an unattended dog.

As with the crate, there is a proper size for a slip collar, which is determined by the size of the pup's neck. I like to have a collar that has no more excess length to it, when drawn snug to the body, than about 3 or 4 inches. To determine the proper size, simply measure the dog's neck a couple of inches behind his ears and add about 3 or 4 inches to that number. This will be the approximate size of the collar you should purchase. Because collars come in even sizes, you may have to round the number up or down to get the right one.

There is a right way and a wrong way to place the slip collar on the pup. The right way allows the collar to release tension more easily and often on its own; the wrong way does not. If you will be training your pup to heel at your left side, then you want to put the slip collar on so that when you and the dog are both facing forward, the collar forms the shape of the letter *p* (think *p* for puppy) as you trace the line of the collar from one ring to another. For the dog trained to heel on your right side, you would have the collar form the shape of the lowercase letter *q*.

LEASH BREAKING

Before you can begin to train a dog on leash, he must accept the leash, much as a horse must learn to

To teach your pup proper behavior on leash, he must first be comfortable wearing his collar with the leash attached.

accept a saddle to be ridden. Begin to leash-break your pup soon after he comes home with you, and do not allow your puppy to learn to pull and tug at the end of the leash. Use a regular buckle collar (no slip collar) for leash breaking.

To begin, attach the leash to the collar, allowing the pup to drag the leash around and get used to the feel of pressure from the leash and collar for a short while before you take hold of the leash and control the dog's ability to roam around. It will be normal for him to pick up the leash and run around with it in his mouth. That is OK, but do not allow the pup to chew on the leash or use it as a toy. All you want to accomplish at this point is to let the dog understand that the feel of the leash and collar is not something to fear.

After a few introductory sessions like this, take hold of the leash and begin to walk with your puppy. If he runs to the end of the leash and begins to pull, you have three choices to make. A bad choice would be to allow him to continue pulling on the leash, for this will make your long-term training program a very difficult road to travel. One good choice is to simply stop moving and let the pup know that as long as he is pulling on the lead, neither of you will be going anywhere. Once he stops pulling, praise him well and start walking again. If he pulls again, repeat the process until he learns that it is simply easier and more fun not to pull on the leash. The other good choice is to simply turn around and start walking the other way when your pup begins to pull, calling him up to you and encouraging him to

move along with you. This is a preferred technique, for it lets the puppy know that you are not out to go where he wants to go but where you do. Using this process also allows you to employ a food lure to entice the puppy back to your side and then to start walking again. If the pup thinks that by staying at or near your side while walking he is likely to end up getting a treat, he will probably walk right next to you on a nice loose leash. If he does not get that idea initially, he soon will.

There are some pups that simply do not want to walk when a leash is attached. These are the pups that, instead of pulling, actually put the brakes on. Dragging them along will sometimes work in the long run, but it will be stressful on you and the pup—not to mention a bit embarrassing for you as the pup is dragged along as though you were doing him bodily harm. To avoid this stressfulness, find out what it will take to entice the dog to move, and use that to draw him into a nice walk. In young pups, food is often a good incentive, but it could also be using a sweet and encouraging voice, patting your hand against your leg to draw him beside you, bringing another dog with you, and so on.

It usually takes only one or two sessions to make the pup comfortable with having a leash attached. Your primary goal is to have the dog understand that he must walk with you without pulling or being dragged along and that to do so is rewarding to him; if you keep that in mind, you should be able to swiftly and successfully conclude this part of your training program.

CORRECTIONS

Although in a utopian world no dog, or human for that matter, would ever have to be corrected or reprimanded for bad behavior or failing to comply with instructions, such is not the case in the real world. Here we all face some form of correction for our failures, and we all come to accept such correction as a normal part of life; the same is true of our dogs. Whether we correct the dog for chewing on our shoes or failing to comply with a command, there will be times when we must let the dog know that he has failed to do the right thing and that he must now face the consequences. Of course, the consequences are seldom very serious, nor do we want them to be, lest we risk making the dog paranoid about his actions.

So when and how do you correct your dog? Your obedience training and many of your field training corrections will contain both a verbal and a physical component. The verbal part is the word *no*, whose meaning was described earlier. The physical part will vary depending on the command or activity being addressed at the time and, at times, on the environment. Of primary importance is the basic tenet that a dog should never be corrected for failure to perform a command he does not understand. This bears repeating: a dog should never be corrected for failure to perform a command he does not understand. If this seems self-evident, I tip my hat to you because this concept has not always made sense to people. Coercive training practices of the past frequently failed to adhere to what we see today as a commonsense understanding.

So rule number one in correcting your dog is never correct until you are sure the dog understands the command and is simply choosing to not comply. I wish I could give you some solid tips on how to identify when that happens, but that is not so easy to do. Yes, you are going to see the dog responding frequently rather than infrequently. Yes, understanding will probably come after days of training rather than simply hours of training. No, the dog's failure to respond to a command will not necessarily be an indication that he does not understand. When I see a dog responding

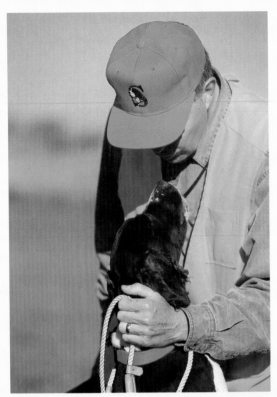
Just as important as corrections is enthusiastic praise for desired responses.

correction that makes the point and gets compliance is going to get you a lot further than a number of little ones that the dog ignores. Remember the point made earlier in this chapter about dogs learning to count? If you nag at the dog with your corrections and do not get compliance until the third or fourth time, you are teaching the dog that he does not have to respond to you right away.

Rule number three says that in the early stages of training you want to give a verbal correction simultaneously with a physical one. This is especially true when training your dog formally with his leash and slip collar attached. The physical correction given with the leash is a swift snap of the collar that imparts a sudden pop to the neck. This gets the dog's attention and is a bit uncomfortable. As the dog progresses, he learns that the way to avoid a correction is to comply with the command. The sequence followed then is this: give a command; if the dog does not comply, say "no" and snap the leash and collar; repeat the command.

When first introducing the corrections, give one good firm reprimand and then repeat your command and show the dog, through the use of a food lure or physical placement, what you want

more often than not without any form of inducement and with general eagerness, I usually believe that he knows what is expected. If you get to the point where you feel sure that the pup has formed an understanding of the command, then you are probably assessing the situation correctly.

Rule number two is that your correction should be swift and matter-of-fact, as opposed to late and nagging. One swift and firm

him to do. As you progress, if the dog fails to comply with the first correction, then give another to a maximum of three corrections before showing the dog what is expected. If your corrections are swift and firm from the beginning, you will probably find that correcting more than once or twice is not necessary.

Finally, despite the fact that you had to correct your dog, when he finally performs the command you gave him, praise, praise, praise. The constant doling out of praise will subside a bit as you progress along with any command, but it is essential to the early stages of teaching any command or action. What you want is for the pup to be performing the task because it is rewarding to do so rather than because of the consequences of failure. So, even if you have to reprimand first, praise the dog when he finally does what he is told to do.

Teaching the Commands

RELEASE

As you begin the training process, you need to adopt an understanding that from now on, when your dog is given a command that he fully understands, he will be expected to continue to do that command until he is given another command or released from commands altogether. Since this concept seems to confuse some people, let me give you an example. Let's assume that your dog understands the command *hup*. Well, when you tell him to *hup*, he needs to do just that, and he needs to remain hupped until he is told to do something else (perhaps a down or heel) or he is released. It is not acceptable for the dog to simply hup and then take off running around the yard or field. If you allow the dog to decide just how long he has

The *hup* command is easily learned and thus is one of the first commands taught.

Steady in the hup position, waiting for the next command, is how most exercises in the field begin.

suggested earlier, and stick to it. Now give the pup a command such as *hup*, and keep him hupped for a short period (fifteen to thirty seconds is fine). Then tell him "free" as you clap your hands, jump up and down, and otherwise carry on like a crazy person. The excitement will cause the pup to break out of the command. Now praise him a bit and go back to having him hup, repeating the hup/free sequence just described. In no time at all, your pup will understand that hearing you say "free," or whatever word you want to use, means that work time is over and that he can go about the business of being a dog.

Hup/Sit

The *hup* command is often the first obedience command taught a dog, and it usually begins, as do many commands, on an informal basis, while you are simply lounging around the house. Part of what makes informal training informal is that you do not need to have either a leash or training collar attached to the dog, and it is done at your leisure. To teach *hup*, get a small treat (as mentioned earlier, a small piece of the pup's kibble is fine), and with it held firmly between your fingers, move your hand down to be level with the pup's nose as he is standing on all fours. You do not

to adhere to any command, you are turning over control to the dog, and he is training you rather than you training him. That is why having a release word is so important to the training process.

Establishing a release word is a rather easy task. First, pick your word, perhaps the word *free* as was

want the pup jumping or standing on his back legs. As you're holding the treat where the pup can smell and see it, waft it around a bit to get his attention and pique his interest. As he attempts to grab the treat, say "hup" while bringing your hand up just enough to start the pup's nose rising, as though he would be looking at you, and then move your hand back toward the pup's tail, remembering not to raise your hand so high that the pup begins to jump or stand on his back legs. What happens here is that the pup will be raising his nose upward and his head backward, which will make him put his rear end on the ground and hup. I usually find that the faster I move my hand, within reason, the faster the pup will hup and the less likely he will be to jump around. Once the pup is hupped, give him the treat and a nice little "good dog," along with some lavish praise for good measure.

You can also teach your pup to hup by physically placing him in that position. To do this, I like to kneel on the floor next to the pup. After grabbing his collar with one hand, I place the other hand on his rump and push downward as I say "hup," while applying a little backward pressure on the collar. Again, dole out praise and reward in good measure once the pup is in the proper position.

Of these two methods for teaching hup, I have come to prefer the first one because it removes the physicality of the process and depends only upon incentive. I believe that dogs learn faster when there are fewer elements to the process, and the use of a food treat to lure a dog into position and instill a command has the fewest elements involved.

The pleasure of using informal training to instill a basic command such as hup is that it can be done more frequently through the day than is possible during a formal training session. This is especially the case when the training sessions are necessarily short, as they are with a young pup just starting out. In a typical day spent at home with your pup, you will probably have the opportunity to teach hup dozens of times. In contrast, having to go through so many repetitions during a typical ten- or fifteen-minute training session would become monotonous for both of you. If the sessions are boring, neither of you will be much interested in partici-pating, so working on hup before you start your formal training will keep things livelier and more inter-esting when you do.

By the time you begin your more formal training sessions, your pup is likely to have the hup com-

Your dog will likely need a lot of practice with a food lure before he's comfortable getting into the down position on his own.

At this point in the process, you are probably ready to begin using some corrections with the dog to gain follow-through on the *hup* command. Remember to apply a swift and firm snap of the collar as you give the correction "no" and then repeat the *hup* command. A little backward angle on the leash and collar correction will sometimes help draw the pup into the hup position; once he is there, simply praise him and move on to the next command.

DOWN

After a couple of days of working on the *hup* command, begin instructing the dog on how to lie down on command. I suggest having your dog work on *hup* first because teaching him to lie down from a hup is much easier than teaching him to do so from a standing position—after all, in the hup position, the dog is already halfway there. Begin again by taking a treat and placing it firmly between your fingers. With the dog hupped, put the treat in front of his nose and, as you say "down," draw your hand straight down toward the floor and then away from the dog. What you want to happen is for the dog to drop his nose to the floor as he follows your hand, sniffing and trying to grab the treat. Then, when

mand fairly well established in his mind, and there will be little to no need for a food lure or physical contact to get him to hup. However, that does not mean that you cannot use both techniques if you find a need. Although there is little difference in implementing the *hup* command with a food lure while the dog is on a leash, there is a slight difference in using physical contact to get the dog to hup. Instead of grasping the collar with one hand as you push downward on the rump, you will control the collar with the leash by drawing the leash and collar snug (not choking) around the neck and then pushing down on the pup's rump as described earlier in this section.

his nose reaches the floor, you draw your hand away from the dog and along the floor; the pup's natural tendency will be to stretch out on his belly and, voilà, you have your pup in a down.

Occasionally the pup will try to stand as you draw your hand toward the floor or as you move it away after he has dropped his head. If this happens, simply start over by putting the pup back in a hup and following through with the sequence outlined earlier, only this time you can place one hand on the pup's shoulders to gently hold him in place and prevent him from rising.

If you choose to teach the pup to lie down from a standing position, follow the same procedure as described for the *hup*, except this time, once your hand has lured his nose to the floor, draw it back between his front legs. A pup will often fall backward and onto his belly to reach the treat and, thus, you have successfully gotten him into a down position.

Teaching the *down* command can also be done by physically placing the pup in a down. To do this, have the pup hup at your left side and place your left hand on his shoulders so that you're able to control him a bit. Now take your right hand and reach behind his right front leg and across to his left front leg and grab it tightly. Push forward and up against his front legs with your right forearm as you apply downward pressure on his shoulders and say "down." This action will slide his front legs out in front of him and his belly to the floor, putting him into a nice down.

When you are ready to move from informal to formal training, the practice regimen for the down command will likely still involve either a food lure or physical placement to gain compliance with the command. By this stage, though, I am usually using physical placement only as a last resort and getting follow-through with the simple use of a treat. In fact, once I have decided that more formal training sessions are in order, the pup has probably been dropping into the down position without having to go into a hup first. It is at this point that I feel the dog has a good understanding of the command, and I will start giving small corrections for a lack of adherence.

The manner in which a leash correction is given for the *down* is no different than that for the *hup* except that the angle of the correction is toward the floor or ground. To administer such a correction, slide your left hand down the leash to take up any excess slack and shorten the amount of leash between

Your dog must obey your recall command despite the distractions around him.

say "hup." He will likely rise into a hup and can now be given the treat. After many repetitions, you will be able to start extinguishing the use of the treat as a lure and simply draw the dog up with your voice command.

COME

Come is the last of the obedience commands that I find easy to train informally, and it is one that I like to begin early. I have always found that because of their unbound energy and inquisitive nature, young pups are the easiest to train to come on command. Although food lures may work well here to draw the puppy to you, so do a number of other tools such as an excited voice, a little hand clapping, and whistling, to name just a few. Therefore, you have the opportunity to mix up the incentives a bit and vary the routine with the pup, which helps prevent boredom and keeps the puppy tuned in to you.

the collar and your hand. Now snap the leash and collar downward as you say the correction "no" and repeat your command. If, after a few corrections, the pup does not follow through, simply place him in a down and move on. Remember that when you have compliance, praise, praise, praise!

One last suggestion is that once your dog understands *down*, you teach him to return to a hup from the down position. To do this, with the dog in a down position, take a treat and hold it in front of his nose and draw the dog up into a sit by bringing your hand up and a little back above the pup's head. As he raises his head to follow the treat, he will rise; as he does, you should

When you begin to work on *come*, remember, as with any command, to use the dog's name to get his attention and then issue the command. In the beginning, applying a little hand clapping along with a higher-pitched, excited voice when you say "come" will often draw the pup toward you like a rocket. If that happens, praise him lavishly and be sure to have a piece of kibble or other treat handy to give him for coming to you so well. Once you are done rewarding the pup for his successful come, let him go about his business for a while before trying the command again. This is a way of not only teaching the dog how to respond to the command but also teaching him that the command may come at any time, not just when there is a specific and structured training setup in place.

Although the randomness of this method is good fun and very effective, so too are more structured yet still informal training setups. One example of such a setup is what I call the "round robin recall." This recall involves at least two family members or helpers; more can certainly join in. Puppies usually have a blast with this little game, and it helps them learn to respond to multiple people as well as to the command word.

In a round robin, the helpers scatter about the room, each armed with a handful of treats. One person holds the pup firmly while one of the helpers talks to the pup and tries to get him excited, perhaps by enticing him with a squeaky toy or other such object. Once the pup is squirming and trying to get to the helper, the person holding the pup lets him go as the helper gives the

come command. Everyone praises the puppy and helps keep his excitement level high. Now the helper has charge of the puppy and holds him firmly, taking away any toy that may have been given to him, lest he be distracted by it. The next helper now begins to rev up the puppy in much the same manner as the first, and the whole process is repeated. This goes on until the pup has successfully completed about six recalls or appears to be getting bored, whichever happens first.

As with *hup* and *down*, by the time you get to the point of beginning your formal training sessions, the pup will have a fairly good idea of what the *come* command means and, you hope, will be coming to you quickly and eagerly. Here are a couple of tips to avoid having the puppy develop a slow and unenthusiastic recall. As with any command, if you cannot get compliance, do not give the command. Do not stand in the doorway of your home, calling your pup as he chases butterflies in the back yard and completely ignores you. To do so simply tells the pup that there are times when he does not have to come, like when he is having a good time doing something else. In those situations, you need to do something other than calling the pup with the *come* command, such as walking outside and distracting him from whatever he is into so that he focuses on you and goes with you into the house.

Another good rule of thumb is to never punish your dog after you have called him to you. Think about it: would you go swiftly and eagerly to someone if you thought something bad would happen to you? Probably not, and neither will your pup. Now, as a pragmatic person, I know that everyone makes this type of mistake from time to time. We are all human. But you need to be aware that these errors in judgment can adversely affect the outcome of your training. It is my hope that recognition of these potential pitfalls will make you less likely to commit such errors and more likely to realize it when you do. In the end, if

your training has far more positive results than negative ones, you will be successful, so don't beat yourself up over the mistakes that you do happen to make.

When you begin your formal training, you will add another element to the *recall* or *come* command—the action of having the pup hup once he gets to you. The sequence used in giving the command is this: say the dog's name, give the *come* command; when the dog gets to you, give the *hup* command. Why have him hup? Because what we are generally seeking when we call a dog to us is control. We want the dog under our more immediate control rather than running around haphazardly. This allows you to wield a little more control over the dog and makes him more subservient, which is a good thing whenever you need to take control.

Eventually, usually within days of adding the hup element to the recall, your pup will start to hup automatically when he comes to you. Wait a few more days, and then begin to extinguish the use of the word *hup* in the command sequence. Then you should expect the dog to hup when he gets to you, and you should give a small correction if he does not.

Formal training on the *come* command should not begin before

Recall training should start when your pup is young, teaching him a behavior that will be imprinted on his brain for life.

you have taught the dog to stay with relative consistency. To train the *come* in a more formal manner, have the puppy on his leash and collar and then place him in a hup, tell him to stay, and walk away from him as you go to the end of the leash. Now, turn and face your pup, wait a moment, and give him the command to come. Once he gets to you, have him hup and shower him with praise for a job well done.

You may run into a few snags with your *stay* command as you start training the puppy to come on leash. These problems usually result from the dog's anticipating that a *come* command will be given once you reach the end of the leash. For this reason, and a few others to be discussed shortly, you should not always call your dog when you get to the end of the leash. Mix it up instead by sometimes calling him, sometimes returning to him to praise him for staying, and other times simply milling about as you reinforce the stay.

If your pup does not come to you when called and while on leash, the correction is obvious but bears mention here. To correct, you simply snap the leash and collar toward you to help guide the dog in the proper direction. Do not tighten the leash and collar to begin dragging the pup over to you; all that will do

is make the pup leery of the leash, collar, and probably you. A series of repetitive snaps will usually cause a pup to get up and begin moving toward you as you call him in. Remember that you are not there to nag but to get your point across and impress upon the pup that a proper response is not an option but a necessity.

Another little trick to use when calling in a reluctant pup is to give a quick leash correction and then begin to run away backward and enthusiastically call the pup to you. You do not have to run very far back, just enough to get the pup moving and completing the command. As always, once he is there—praise!

When your pup has developed a sound and consistent come from a distance of 6 feet, you can begin to lengthen the distance between the two of you by switching from a 6-foot leash to either a 20-foot long line (a fancy name for a long leash) or a retractable leash, which gives you both control and distance while training your pup.

STAY

I do not like to attempt teaching *stay* until I am ready to begin formal training. *Stay* requires that the dog be both corrected and returned to the spot from which he left to instill a sound understanding of *stay*. Now, as mentioned earlier, generally we do not correct a dog for failure to adhere to a command unless we are certain that the dog understands the command. Well, here is where we break that rule a bit—just a bit. We do correct when a pup fails to stay whether he understands the command or not, but the correction is relatively minor when he is first learning and increases in intensity only as he gains more understanding of the command.

Remember that the dog must learn to stay before moving on to the *come* command during a formal training session, so this command needs to be worked on quickly once you have progressed from the informal to the formal. It is also an important command used by every hunter whether he is hunting upland birds and needs the dog to hup and stay when the bird is flushed or he is hunting ducks over a small decoy spread and needs the dog steady so he does not flare the birds as they draw toward the decoys. Here are a few methods that will help you quickly and easily teach your pup to stay.

With the leash and collar attached to the pup, have him hup at your left side. With both hands on your leash, tell him to stay and step off on your right foot as you im-

mediately turn to face the pup directly in front of him. If he should get up from his hup or otherwise move from his spot, quickly issue a leash correction as you reprimand him with "no." Then repeat the *hup* command, getting him back into a sit, and praise him well but not so much so that he breaks from his hup. If he stays without moving, give him a soft-spoken (you do not want to cause him to move by giving a lot of vigorous praise) "good dog" and step back to his right side. Reach down and give him a pet or two and repeat the exercise.

After you can do this minor exercise with the pup, begin to work yourself farther from him after stepping out in front. Begin by taking one step backward; on each step you will tell the pup "hup. . . stay." Remember to praise him if he stays and to correct him if he moves.

Once you begin to step farther from the pup, you do not need to always return to his side when he has been corrected or praised. In fact, you want to mix things up a bit, and to that end you will sometimes return to his side, sometimes call him to you with the "come" command, and sometimes simply have him begin to heel at your side.

Once you can routinely tell the pup to stay and walk to the end of the leash without much chance of his moving, begin to introduce a little more distraction. Distractions help make the pup's stays more reliable by teaching him that if he moves because of some commotion around him, he will be corrected. The more he understands this and the more he wishes to both avoid a correction and receive a reward, the more likely he is to remain in position no matter what.

The first distractions introduced will simply be your moving about at the end of the leash. I have been known to dance a jig once I get to the end of the leash and then begin walking in circles around the dog as I constantly praise and reinforce the command with a pleasant "hup . . . stay." Other distractions that can be introduced to the mix over time— not early on—are other people walking by, children riding their bicycles past you, throwing a tennis ball in a way that entices him to chase, and so forth. If you think that something in particular may distract him from his stay, then try to set up the situation in which that distraction is introduced while he is practicing the stay. If you do all of this, you will end up with a spaniel who is a steady flushing dog capable of nonslip retrieving.

I have not mentioned much here about using food rewards for the

Begin teaching the stay command standing close to your dog, increasing your distance from him gradually.

stay command, but that is not because I do not use them. Early in the process, I often use food as a reward for a good stay by occasionally returning to the pup when he has stayed and reaching down to him with a treat in hand while repeating the command "hup . . . stay" as I let him take the treat. I often add a little pat on the head and a rub of his back for good measure.

Furthermore, although I have suggested that you begin to work on *stay* in conjunction with the *hup* command, you should also incorporate the *down* into this process.

Before formal heel training begins, your pup must be comfortable on his leash.

training, you will have accustomed the dog to the leash and trained him to hup on command. As with all previously discussed commands, I like to begin this process indoors and away from distractions, although heeling does not lend itself to training in most living rooms.

Your goal here is not to simply teach the dog to walk at your side but to teach him to do so on a loose leash while he pays attention to both you and his surroundings. If you have ever watched competitive obedience dogs, you have seen how many of them are practically wrapped around their handlers legs, nearly impeding the free movement of the handlers; they focus more on the handlers' legs and body movement than on what is happening around them. We do not want this in the field dog. A field dog should not interfere or even come close to interfering with you as you move through a field. He should have the ability to focus on the surroundings, ready for a possible flush or to mark an incoming bird such as a duck that may be flying into the decoy spread as you sneak closer to the pothole.

Begin heel training when you feel that the dog is accustomed to walking with you on leash and when he has completed the preliminary work on *hup*, *down*, and

The steps are no different other than that you will be replacing *hup* with down. However, it can be more difficult to get a pup to stay in the *down* position initially than to stay sitting, so for the first week or so I would stick with the *hup/stay* before moving on to the *down/stay* command.

HEEL

"Heeling" your dog simply refers to having your dog walk at your side— your heel, if you will—rather than out in front of you or behind you. By the time you get to this stage of *come*. This is the point at which you are moving out to your garage or down to your basement, where you have more room to work with the pup and you can avoid a lot of distractions. Be sure to have the leash and collar properly placed on the dog, and start by having the dog hup at your left side. Before you begin to walk, step yourself into what is commonly referred to as the "heel position": the dog sitting at your left side with his right shoulder aligned with your left leg. Be sure that you have two hands holding the leash properly and that there is slack in the leash and collar.

Now get your pup's attention, perhaps with a treat or simply your voice, so he focuses on you for a few seconds. This increases the likelihood that he will recognize what is coming next and not be surprised when you walk off, leaving him sitting there. Once you have his attention, step off on your left foot (that is the one closest to the dog) as you give the command "pup, heel" and begin walking. If you have been walking him on leash, he will probably start walking with you and follow along. He may not walk exactly where you want him to, but when he does walk, you want to praise, praise, praise.

After a short distance—no more than a dozen steps—stop and tell the pup to hup. Why hup? For the same reason we have the pup hup when he comes to us. You want control. Eventually, your pup will learn that whenever he is heeling and you come to a stop, he is to hup and hup quickly, but for now you need to give the command and lay the foundation for this behavior to become automatic. The reason for taking just a few short steps is because you want to ease the dog into an understanding that he must always properly heel with you and not wander off. Asking a pup that is just starting out with a new command to stay focused on that command for more than a few seconds is unreasonable. As you progress with your training, you can lengthen the distance before changing gears, but do so over time, taking a few days to get to the point of being able to heel the pup for more than two or three minutes without a change in focus.

Although your pup is likely to follow along when you first begin to heel him, it is also likely that he is not going to be in the exact position you want him to be in. Your job is to get him there and to make him want to be there more so than anywhere else. The best way to accomplish this is for the pup to understand that when his shoulder is aligned with your body, all is right in the world; when it is not, the world is a little less pleasant. As you begin to train to heel, I suggest that you have a few treats easily accessible and that you occasionally give him a treat as he walks along in the proper heel position. Bring the treat down to the pup's level to prevent him from jumping up for the treat, and give it to him with your left hand to avoid having him jump in front of you as he looks for another treat. Carrying on a pleasant conversation with your dog while he is properly heeling will also serve to keep him in the correct position.

Your dog will leave the heel position at your side to go out for retrieves.

Although it would be wonderful to teach a pup to heel properly without ever having to correct him for leaving the heel position, the chance of this happening is about as good as the chance of my winning the lottery. Correcting is inevitable and necessary, so be prepared for this eventuality. There are some pretty common ways in which pups tend to leave the heel position, and each has its own correction with which you should familiarize yourself with before you begin to teach the pup to heel.

I believe the most common error that a pup makes is to try to walk forward of the proper position. The best correction is to simply make an abrupt turn in the opposite direction as you give the dog a little slack in the leash. If the pup is paying attention, he will quickly turn and follow along, getting back into the heel position, where you can eagerly praise him as he does. Should the pup not be paying attention, he will quickly hit the end of the leash, and you will then give him a few jerks of the leash and draw it up to you as you encourage him to get back into position.

The opposite of the dog that forges ahead of you is the dog that wants to lag behind. Why some dogs want to forge ahead and others lag behind is sometimes anyone's guess, but this is a problem that can be induced rather than a product of the dog's mental makeup. Too many corrections at your side or somehow having an unpleasant experience at your side will cause this problem quicker than you care to know. A lagging dog needs a lot of encouragement and reward for doing it right. You can still give short gentle jerks on the leash to draw him into the correct position, but be cautious of overdoing it. Whatever you do, do not adjust your pace to meet that of the dog's, for doing so will simply make the pup lag behind you more, not to mention the fact that the dog will become the teacher and you the student. Keep up your pace, and do a lot of encouraging to bring the dog into the proper position.

Some dogs will crowd your leg while heeling. This is often a sign of anxiousness, perhaps brought on by too much correcting and not enough praise, or it may simply be the result of the dog's mental makeup; whatever the reason, you need to go easy because this dog is in a sensitive state. I find that the best way of correcting this behavior is to simply turn into the dog and push him away with your left leg whenever he crowds you. Once the dog is off your leg and out of the way, give a lot of praise and move on. After a while, a dog like this will simply give up on the crowding and accept staying in the proper position.

The opposite of crowding you is pulling away or swinging out to the left. Much like forging ahead, this is an easy one to fix by turning sharply to the right and taking a 90-degree turn away from the dog. As with forging ahead, you give a little extra slack in the leash and correct the pup quickly if he does not come back into the heel position soon. Remember to praise when he is where you want him to be.

As you progress with your pup's training, you will be moving outdoors, where there are more distractions, such as blowing leaves, kids playing in the yard, other dogs running by, an occasional squirrel running up a tree, and myriad other things to interfere with your training. These are good things to train around, as they will help solidify your dog's ability to heel under the most arduous of conditions. Do not shy from such opportunities, but do take your time with them and simply make your dog do the work that is necessary.

PLACE

The *place* command is one of the handiest commands that you can teach your dog and, like most commands, it is applicable to both field and home situations. A house dog taught to respond to this command can be sent to his place during dinnertime, when there is a visitor at the door, or at any other time you find it beneficial to have the dog out of the way but not necessarily confined to his kennel. A field dog taught the *place* command will have less trouble becoming steady, either in the upland fields or when working as a nonslip retriever.

As with all commands, you begin your *place* training indoors and gradually move outside. *Place* is an extension of the *stay* command, and I do not recommend that you begin teaching it until the dog has a solid understanding of *stay*. To make your job easier and the dog's learning go more quickly, you will need to have a target that the dog can identify as his place. You can use a dog bed, an old towel, or my personal favorite, one of those carpet samples you can often buy at your local home-improvement store. Make sure that the target is easily distinguished from other objects. For instance, if you are going to use a carpet sample and you will be putting it on top of your family room carpet, make certain that the two carpets are of contrasting colors and textures.

When you begin your training, you will establish a set location for the target item, but eventually you will move the item around and, thus, change the location of the dog's place from time to time. This is a necessary step in teaching a field dog the *place* command. He needs to know that his place may change but that your expectations for him will not.

To teach *place*, take your dog near the target—a distance of no more than 6 feet away is fine—and draw his attention to it by patting the target as you repeatedly say "place." If the dog goes to the spot, praise him and have him hup. Now tell him to stay, and back away from the target for a brief moment. Return to the pup and give him a lot of praise before you release him. If the pup is not drawn to the target as you pat it, then try luring him with a treat, much as you would lure him to come to you. Once the pup is on the target, give him the treat and praise. Tell him "hup," then "stay," and after a short time release him, praising profusely.

If all else fails and you just cannot get the pup to walk to the target, pick him up and put him there. Try to avoid doing this, however. You want to teach the dog to go to his place on his own, not by being carried every time. Eventually your dog will pick up on the idea that the command "place" means that he should get to his spot, where he will be rewarded for doing so. As with all commands, you will extinguish the use of the reward in time and will simply expect the dog to comply.

Because this command is begun indoors, it can be worked on at any randomly selected time of the day. The more often the better, and the quicker your dog will learn this command. Once he has the command down inside the house, move to the garage or basement, and make this a part of your normal training routine. Simply pick up the target (another good reason for using old carpet samples), take it to the garage, and throw it down near where you will be training. As before, pat the target and repeat the command "place" a few times to let the dog know where his place is. From time to time during your session, send the dog to his place and keep him there for a short time before moving on to another command. When it comes time to move outside and face greater distractions, you will follow the same routine you've established.

Remember that the *place* command is one that keeps the dog anchored in a specific spot or area but allows him to move around a bit to be comfortable. Although we start to teach this command by getting the dog to the spot and

You can use your dog's bed as his "place" when teaching this command.

having him sit-stay, we eventually extinguish the added *sit-stay* command from the training sequence. This allows the dog to move around freely in his place. Correcting the pup on this command is done only if he fails to go to his spot and stay.

To correct the dog, physically take the dog to his place and firmly give him the *place* command again. If you see him attempting to leave his place, then give him a firm "no" and repeat the *place* command, followed by praise when he follows through. Avoid physically correcting him in his place because you do not want him to associate anything unpleasant with this spot. Think of it much as an invisible kennel. We want him to want to be there and to be comfortable with being there, not fearful of what might happen when he is in his place.

The spaniel whistle is good for close work, and the retriever whistle for commanding your dog at a distance.

MIXING IT UP

As has been mentioned in some of these training descriptions, you want to have training sessions that combine the various commands, allowing you to cover all of them several times each and requiring that the dog stay focused in order to complete each task properly. Once you have gotten to the point of formally training everything from the simple *hup* to the *heel* command, you will have enough variety to allow you to have an intense fifteen- to twenty-minute training session two or three times each day. To help you understand what I mean when I say "mix it up," let me give you a

rundown of a typical training sequence that lists the commands given in a random order. Such a list might look like this: hup—stay—come—heel—down—hup—stay—heel—down—heel—stay—down—hup—come—and so forth. Keep the variety in your sessions, and you will maintain the pup's focus, not to mention yours.

WHISTLES

If you want a well-controlled and responsive gundog, start training your pup on whistle commands soon after graduating to more formal training sessions. Why use a whistle when your voice can work just as well or better? Because the sound of the whistle can carry over greater distances than your voice can, and it can break through the background sounds that, at times, saturate the dog's brain. Besides, I would much rather listen to a whistle being blown to control a dog than some frustrated handler screaming his lungs out.

The type of whistle you choose to use will likely be predicated on your personal preference and a bit of peer pressure. When it comes to training flushing dogs, most trainers will use either a spaniel whistle, which typically has a high soft pitch, or a retriever whistle with a deep harsh sound; I use both. I prefer the spaniel whistle for close-in work, when the dog is working a meadow or woodlot. Because the dog is in close, I do not need the sound to carry in the manner that a retriever whistle does. If the dog is being used to hunt waterfowl and may need to be controlled at a great distance or is surrounded by the sound of water as he swims, I will use a retriever whistle. The only times I tend to use a retriever whistle for close-in control is when the wind has kicked up, making it difficult to hear clearly. Otherwise, I find the retriever whistle to be unnecessarily noisy.

Although there will be a few additional whistle signals added later in this book, we will begin with just the *come-in* and *hup* whistles for right now. I do not like to incorporate whistle commands into the training process too early because I prefer to build a more solid foundation first. Once I have gotten a pup to the point of understanding and readily responding to the basic verbal command, I add the whistle element to the equation.

The standard whistle command used to tell a dog to hup is one moderately long pip on the whistle: *tweeeet*. Introduce the whistle command during your formal on-leash training sessions. To begin, you will give the whistle command

The *hup* whistle is one of the basic whistle commands, with others introduced later in the training process.

(*tweeeet*) followed right away by the verbal command (*hup*) and then by a lot of praise if the dog complies or a correction (*no, hup*) if he does not. If the dog truly understands *hup*, the odds are in your favor that he will comply.

Continue with this sequence for a number of days, until you begin to see consistently that the dog is going into a hup right after he hears the whistle command. Once this occurs, you can begin to extinguish the use of the verbal command in the command sequence and switch to just the whistle signal. From this point on, you will need to mix up the two signals from time to time by sometimes giving the verbal command and at other times giving simply the whistle command. Just remember that no matter which signal you give, you must demand compliance.

The *come* whistle is taught in the same manner as the hup whistle, but the signal is usually a series of pips, something like *tweet-tweet-tweet-tweet-tweet*. It really does not matter how many times or in what way you blow your whistle as long as you are consistently giving the same signal to the dog time after time.

In the Field

I once owned a pointer (I will not say what breed of pointer) from top field trial stock. He was a beautiful animal, and his pedigree made any field trial man envious. The story behind how I ended up with this dog is immaterial here, but I had not gotten him with the intention of having him as a field dog, so I really did not care about pedigree or if he would hunt. I had taken him in at the age of nine months to save his life and give him a home. However, as I am an ardent hunter, I figured that I would let him tag along on some training excursions and the occasional hunting trip. Surely, with his pedigree, he was going to be a fine hunting dog—or so I thought.

From the first day he set foot in a field that was not mowed smooth, he showed that he wanted nothing to do with busting brush, skirting under old fences, or jumping over downed trees. Had I bought him as a hunting dog, I would have been extremely disappointed, but he proved to be a nice companion for my wife while I was away on hunting trips. So why did this dog not like being in the woods and meadows? I think it was because he had never been introduced to cover at a young age. He had been primarily raised in a boarding kennel from about two months of age and never had to face the complexities of a day afield. Why should he have to do so at the age of nine or ten months?

No matter how much potential your dog may have as a result of his genes or innate characteristics, it is your responsibility to get him out to the fields two or three times a week and let him explore those environments that will surely make up his working life. Let him plow through tall grasses, dig under brambles, and run through creeks. Let him sniff out mice, check out rabbit dens, and chase butterflies or songbirds to his heart's content. In short, let your pup be a pup; in so doing, you will be ingraining in him a love for the outdoors and a level of comfort that will forever remain at his core.

As you get your pup out into the fields and take him for walks through cover, meander through these areas in a back-and-forth, crisscrossing pattern that mimics the way you will one day have your pup working through a field. As you change direction, give two short pips (*tweet-tweet*) on the whistle and encourage your dog to follow you. In short order, you will have your dog not only accustomed to cover but also starting to catch on to the fact that *tweet-tweet* means "turn and head in the other direction" (more on this later).

RETRIEVING

One of the primary building blocks of a good hunting spaniel is his ability to tirelessly retrieve. The steps you take to properly train your puppy to retrieve will make the entire process go much more smoothly, and you will avoid the common pitfalls that besiege a lot of new puppy owners.

Most of us begin training our puppies with what are commonly referred to as play retrieves. These retrieves rely less on a structured training format and more on the pup's natural tendencies to chase and pick up objects in his mouth as well as his desire to be with you. A pup that is not demonstrating any one of these natural traits will

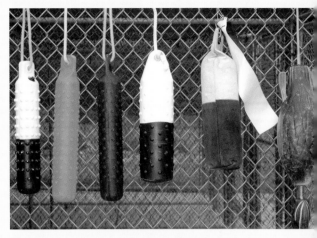

There are a variety of types of retrieving dummies available to the trainer.

probably have a problem even with play retrieves. Therefore, before you begin to give the puppy some play retrieves, ask yourself whether the pup has been demonstrating these three basic elements and, if not, delay starting this work until he does exhibit these traits.

Start your pup's retrieving with the use of a small canvas puppy bumper, which is about half to two-thirds the size of a normal bumper. Before starting to throw the bumper for the puppy, you want him to become a bit acquainted with this new object, so encourage him to sniff and grab the bumper while you keep a firm grip on it. Do not simply give the puppy the bumper yet because there is a risk that the pup will just grab it and run off, setting a bad precedent for future training. If the pup is not quite interested in the bumper, try rubbing your hands all over the bumper and thus imparting your scent on it. This sometimes makes a pup more willing to grab the bumper. Once the puppy seems comfortable with the bumper and has shown some interest it, move ahead.

Take hold of the pup's collar with one hand so that you can control him and, with the other hand, begin to tease him with the bumper. How do you tease the puppy? Wave the bumper around in front of him, get excited with both your voice and your physical actions, tap the bumper on the ground, and do anything else you can think of to make the puppy want to dive on the bumper. When you believe you have the pup suffi-ciently excited, give the bumper a little toss a few yards away and release your puppy, calling his name as you do. (His name will become the word you use to send him on a marked retrieve.) In all likelihood, he is going to run to the bumper and snatch it up. As soon as he does, start clapping your hands, praising him, and calling him back to you. When he comes back with the bumper, and most pups will come back quickly, give him a lot of praise and let him hold on to or play with the bumper for a

couple of minutes. After a sufficient amount of time has passed, take the bumper from the puppy and repeat this process for two more throws, but no more. You do not want to do too many retrieves at this point, or you risk boring the puppy and wearing him down. It is always best to leave the puppy wanting more.

Now what has just been described is the ideal response to that first toss of the bumper, but what happens if the response you get is less than ideal? What sort of problems might you encounter, and how do you fix them?

A common problem is that the dog does not come back to you but runs off somewhere with his bumper. There are two steps that you can take to prevent this. One is to have a leash attached to the pup that you can grab and use to guide him to you once he has picked up the bumper. If you need to resort to using a leash, be sure to gently guide the puppy toward you as you en-courage him to cooperate and, of course, praise him profusely when he gets there, letting him have the bumper for a short while before taking it away. Another technique is to conduct your play retrieve in a confined area where there is no means of escape and where you are the best thing going. This often means giving your pup his play retrieves down a hallway, with all the adjoining doors closed to cut off escape routes.

Another problem that surfaces with a beginning pup is when a puppy gets all excited over the teasing with the bumper but after the throw he simply runs out to the bumper, sniffs it, and then walks away. This may spell real trouble or it may simply indicate that the pup is not quite ready for this work. If this happens, go pick up the bumper, then call the puppy over to you and start again with the teasing and the short toss. Should the puppy continue to show a lack of interest, stop the activity and try again later, usually right after the pup has had a good rest. I have had some pups take as many as four or five sessions before they suddenly began to pick up the bumper, so do not despair too early. However, if this continues for too long and you just don't seem able to get the pup interested in picking up a bumper, you need to call in a pro for help.

Although some pups don't show much interest in a bumper right away, others are so excited that they get to the bumper and start to chew on it or toss it around while refusing to bring it to you. The solution here is to walk over and take the bumper away. Then put a leash on the pup

and toss the bumper again. This time when the pup reaches the bumper, give him a little time—two or three seconds—to decide what to do, and if he chooses not to return to you, start to reel him in. You

The goal is for the dog to willingly give you the bumper, not drop it before he reaches you or run off and play with it.

Some pups just can't wait to begin retrieve training!

cannot let the pup believe that he can sit and chew the bumper or refuse to come to you. So take the steps necessary to get him back.

If you are reeling a puppy like this in to you and he drops the bumper, do not worry. Your primary goal at this point is to let the little pup know that you want him to come back to you and not to play this game. After you reel him in, if he has dropped the bumper, go pick it up so that you can try again. Eventually the pup will learn to keep a firm grip on the bumper and to return to you right away.

Some trainers believe that the use of a food treat will help get the pup coming back to you right away. This may be true, but I have found that the food treat usually causes the pup to drop the bumper in antici-

pation of getting the treat. For this reason, I do not recommend using a food reward on this exercise.

Remember that we start this process in much the same way as we do with obedience training, that is, in a confined area with few distractions. Once the pup has demonstrated that he will readily retrieve a bumper to you each and every time in this type of setting, you can begin to introduce the common distractions found around the home. Take the pup out to the back yard and toss a few retrieves as the kids play nearby, your neighbor mows his lawn, or the squirrels chase each other up and down trees. If you have trouble controlling the pup without a leash, then keep a leash on him so that you can maintain control and success. Better to have success with a leash than failure without one.

After several days of moving about the yard and providing a mixture of distractions for the pup, begin lengthening the retrieves. Expand the distance that you throw the bumper in small but ever-increasing increments. If you hit a distance at which you have trouble, then stay there until you have worked through the problems; if you don't, they will only get worse as you make the retrieves longer.

This is also the time to begin using a whistle command to call the dog back in to you with the bumper. You can use the same signal that is used for the *come* command (*tweet-tweet-tweet-tweet-tweet*), or you can use something different; just be consistent with your signal.

BIRDS

When it comes to experiencing new things, does your pup boldly go forward, or does he take a more cautious approach? Answer this question honestly, because the answer will determine how you approach bird introduction. If you are not quite sure, then take the approach suggested below for a cautious pup.

Ideally, you will not begin bird introduction until you are sure that your pup is comfortable with cover and will come to you when called or, better yet, reliably retrieve for a pup of his age. Of course, that is the ideal, but when you decide that you cannot wait for the ideal time to develop, you will probably go forward, thinking that it surely can't hurt. As a pragmatic person, I understand that these things happen; just realize that once you have this out of your system, you need to go back to basics and finish the job of early retrieve training and properly introducing your pup to cover

before pushing ahead and working with more birds.

For the pup that faces new challenges with a bit of trepidation, take bird introduction slowly, and begin with a dead bird placed strategically among a bit of short cover where the pup is sure to wander and come across this new discovery. Use a small bird, such as a pigeon or a chukar, that will be easily handled by a young pup. When the pup crosses paths with the bird, his reaction will be somewhere between a bit of fright at this new discovery and determined self-confidence as he sniffs, jumps at, and pulls at the bird. If you are lucky, the pup will actually pick up the bird and begin to drag it away, laying claim to this new find. Should this happen, call the pup to you and start praising him profusely for finding such a wonderful thing. As you did with your early retrieving adventures, do not take the bird away from the pup right away; let him savor his new find for a few minutes as you continue to praise him for a job well done.

The pup that does not readily pick up the bird may simply need some time to study it further. As long as he is showing interest in the bird, let him continue to do whatever he wants with the bird and simply watch what is happening,

Take time to give your pup a pleasant introduction to birds, as it will pay off later with a reliable retriever in the field.

doing nothing to interfere. If the pup loses interest and moves on, then just grab the bird and put it away for another day or for your next walk in cover. Most well-bred hunting spaniel pups will take to the bird in short order; if he doesn't, just keep trying this introduction until he does.

For the really bold pup that throws caution to the wind and dives full bore into all new adventures, you can use a taped-wing pigeon or chukar rather than a dead bird. I warn you here, though, because a pup that is not bold and displays cautiousness when facing

new events might get frightened enough of birds to turn off to them completely. As I wrote earlier, if you are in doubt about your pup's reaction, then use only a dead bird when introducing the pup to birds for the first few times.

What I like about using a taped-wing bird with a new pup is that it often turns on the pup's prey drive as it moves around, sometimes running and sometimes attempting to fly. With the prey drive kicked in, the pup is frequently more willing to attempt to pick up the bird and, indeed, often does grab the bird and carry it. When that happens, we know we have the pup hooked on his instinctive qualities, and we can be optimistic about his future as a hunting dog.

GUNFIRE

I have never had a problem introducing pups to gunfire, but I know of a lot of people who have. Their stories are often the same: the owner took the pup to the local gun range, where he could hear the sound of gunfire, or he took the pup out to the countryside and fired off a round just to see how the dog would react. When the pup ran under the car or hid behind the owner's legs, the owner was surprised because, after all, his pup was from well-titled stock. Titles in a pedigree do not assure much when it comes to fear of gunfire, especially when the gunfire is introduced improperly.

I do not believe in banging away at pots and pans, banging small slabs of wood together, or any of the other ideas that have been used over the years to supposedly accustom a pup to the sound of gunfire or loud noises in general. What I do believe in is a gradual introduction to the sound of a gunshot and making a connection between that sound and whatever it is the pup finds pleasurable. Furthermore, I believe that the only important sound here is that of a gun. Two pieces of wood slapped together do not create a sound much like a gun, nor do pots and pans banged together; however, a training pistol (especially one set up to fire shotgun primers) comes close enough that, when used properly, it will lead toward success.

The best place to introduce your pup to gunfire is in the field. The best time to introduce a gunshot is when the pup is focused on chasing a bird and a bit oblivious to all the other things going on around him. Do not fire a gunshot when you are in close proximity to the pup but when you are a good 20 or 30 yards away. If

To a seasoned hunting dog, the sound of gunfire is just part of a day's work.

your pup will not get that far away from you, then enlist some help. Have a friend walk well behind you with the training pistol as you take your pup through the field. Work out a signal that you will give your friend to let him know that it is time to fire off a shot.

As you and the pup walk the field, watch for him to begin chasing a songbird or a taped-wing

Wet and wide-eyed, a future water retriever gets his start.

there is a bird to be retrieved, and gunshots will become extremely exciting to him.

WATER

It may seem strange to the average person, but not all dogs take to water well. Whether it simply is not in their nature or the result of a bad experience, some dogs just do not enjoy going for a swim. If you have such a dog, either accept what you have and make the most of it or try working with a professional trainer to see if such intervention might help the situation. There are no guarantees, however.

I start water introduction very early on. In fact, when I raise a litter of pups and the weather is right, they are at the pond around the age of five weeks, and many are swimming well before they ever leave my kennel at eight weeks of age. Water introduction should be a planned-out affair consisting of numerous trips to water and gradually increasing expectations or opportunities. Here are some elements that you need to factor into your planning.

Make sure that the water is comfortable for the pup. Water that is too cold will turn the pup off right away. If you are living in the north, conduct your water introduction between late April

bird that you planted before bringing the pup out into the field. As he begins to chase, pull out your training pistol and fire a shot—just one shot—or signal your friend to do it for you. Watch the pup's reaction. If he seemed to ignore the shot and especially if he continued to chase the bird, you can do this again later. If he reacted to the shot by running back to you, then wait another few days or a week before attempting it again. Eventually, he will come to ignore the shot and simply go on about his business. As he matures, he will actually come to understand that a gunshot means

and late October, depending upon the particular year and your area's specific climate, of course.

The best water to start out in is a wide body of shallow water in which the pup can romp without having to swim right away. A firm bottom that allows the pup to feel as if he has sure footing is also best. Slow-moving streams or creeks, particularly wide ones, often work well for this process. You can also use flooded fields in the spring and fall, where broad yet shallow expanses of water often form and provide the perfect setting for water introduction.

You are a key element in the process, and getting your pup into water will go faster if you go in with him. By the time you are ready to work on water intro-duction, your pup should be well bonded to you and wanting to be with you above all else. As you walk through a shallow expanse of water and head to the opposite side, the pup is going to have a big incentive to follow you, as he will not want to be left behind. Although his mind may be telling him to be wary of the water, his need to stay with you will often be the overriding force that drives him through the water and out to you.

When it is time to begin, take the pup to the site you have chosen and walk him around the area near the water's edge; do not have a leash attached to the pup. Slowly work your way into the shallows, and walk parallel to the shore. As the puppy follows, encourage him to come into the water with you, and praise him when he does. Encouragement can take many forms, from luring with food treats to speaking in a high-pitched and inviting voice to simply sitting down in the shallows and letting your pup climb all over you. Once the pup comes to the shallows, continue to wade around with him, letting him wander but keeping him from going into deep water too soon. This could be the extent of your first venture into water, but if your pup is particularly bold, you may decide to continue on.

Next, when your pup will easily play in the shallows of a stream, pond, or flooded area, take him to a similar area with a small section of water deep enough for him to have to swim but not so deep that you will have to swim as well. Walk into the water with the pup, wade in the shallows for a bit, and then head toward the deeper water with the pup following along. Head right through the area of deep water so that the pup has to momentarily swim if he is to stay with you. The puppy may turn and head away from you when he feels that he has lost his footing, but you should simply keep on walking, encouraging him to follow, and wait for him on the other side of the deep water area. If you are in an area where the pup can run out and around to get to you, then simply stand in the middle of the deeper part of the water and encourage the pup to come to you. As he does, praise him as though he just helped you win the lottery and continue on. Return to this site or one much like it several times until your pup is swimming with confidence and no hesitation.

It is now time to move to a different source of water, one where the pup will have to rely more on his swimming ability and less on his wading ability. The water here should still be shallow enough for you to wade into and through just in case you need to go in and provide some security for the pup. You can now take along a bumper for the puppy to retrieve.

Walk the pup down to the water's edge and wade around for a few minutes as described earlier. Pull out the bumper and tease him with it a little. Although he is wading around, toss the bumper just a few feet away, but preferably not into water in which the pup will have to swim. When he goes for and grabs the bumper, praise

him and signal him to bring it back to you. Praise him again when he returns to you with the bumper. Toss the bumper a few more times in this manner, and then make a final toss out into deeper water that will cause the pup to have to swim. Just make sure that the toss is not too long. Your goal here is not to get a long retrieve (although that is always a good thing) but to get the puppy swimming in deep water. If the retrieve is too long, the pup may balk at going all the way to the bumper, which will set up failure. You want successes, so try to keep the retrieves short, no more than several yards in length.

After that one retrieve in which the pup had to swim, end your session. Come back to this spot the next time and do it all again, but this time toss only a couple of retrieves into shallow water before expanding out to the deeper water. Keep the number of retrieves to four to six and the distances relatively short. As time goes on, stop throwing the shallow-water retrieves and move right into the deep-water retrieves, adding more distance each time. You have now successfully introduced your pup to water and have a dog that will not hesitate to retrieve a bird that falls in a pond, creek, lake, or marsh.

Some dogs truly immerse themselves in their water retrieves.

Being able to retrieve birds from the water is one of
the criteria of what's termed a *started dog*.

Chapter 6

The
Started Dog

By this point in your training, you have molded your pup into a nice little companion and started him on the path toward becoming a finished gundog, but he is yet to turn into what one may call a started dog. That term, *started dog*, tends to come with numerous definitions, so it is best if we define the term as it is used in this book.

A started dog is one that is:
- obedient to both verbal and whistle commands
- trained to quarter a field in search of game
- accustomed to gunfire and has been shot over
- experienced at retrieving birds from land and water

In short, a started dog is one that is ready to hit the field for a day's hunt but trained only in the fundamentals. Such a dog is not yet capable of addressing any of the more complex issues that can arise in the field and would be easily dealt with by a dog with greater experience and training. You and practically any hunting companion would be happy to take a started dog out for a day of pheasant, dove, or duck hunting.

Lightweight plastic bumpers, appropriate for the size of your pup or dog, are best for practice on the water.

This chapter is intended to carry you further along in the training process and help you develop the pup into a started dog.

Getting the Right Equipment

RETRIEVING BUMPERS

Retrieving bumpers come in a variety of sizes and colors. Generally speaking, you will work with a white canvas bumper that is about 3 inches by 12 inches when working on land and a white plastic bumper that is 2 inches by 12 inches when doing water work. The white color usually makes the bumper easier to see both on the ground and in the air. Colored bumpers are sometimes used to increase the difficulty level of the retrieve and for training a dog on blinds (retrieving objects that the dog did not see fall). Under some conditions, a colored bumper may be best to use against a specific background. For instance, if you are throwing a white bumper on a sunny day with a bright blue sky as the background, the dog may not see it well. Using a black bumper in this situation would make it easier for the dog to see the mark as it rises and falls and thus be better for the dog. You can buy bumpers with one black end and one white end. I like these because it usually means that the dog will be able to see the bumper under any condition. You can find orange, yellow, blue, and other colored bumpers, all of which have some advantage but none of which is necessary to own.

Bumpers are also made from a variety of materials, including canvas, plastic, and urethane. The plastic bumpers are the best for use on the water because their weight allows for an easier and longer throw and, more important, they float. They can be used in the field as well, but I still prefer the canvas models there just so the dogs have some variety. Variety is also why I try to have a few jumbo bumpers around. These have a wider diameter of about 4 inches and come in both plastic and canvas. They require the dog to carry more weight and open his mouth wider. In short, larger bumpers are a bit more in line with retrieving an actual bird.

The most realistic bumpers for training are the urethane foam bumpers, often referred to as "Dokkens" after the original brand, Dokken Dead Fowl Trainers. These bumpers look and feel like the real thing. In fact, you order them by the type of bird you want to train for. Once a pup has completed his basic field training, I use these bumpers almost exclusively and most certainly on water retrieves.

I recommend that your training supplies include:

- one puppy bumper (optional)
- twelve white/black 3" x 12" canvas bumpers
- six white/black 2" x 12" plastic bumpers
- three each 4" x 12" white/black canvas and plastic bumpers
- six urethane foam bumpers of your preferred style

BELT AND CHECK CORDS

The belt and check cords are used to control the pup at your side and to ease any transition that must take place when the pup is progressing from on-leash to off-leash training. Although you have read about the check cord (or long line) already, I have not yet mentioned the belt cord. This is because this cord is specific to teaching your dog to work as a nonslip retriever—in other words, having him steady by your side or at the line.

Whereas a check cord is long, the belt cord is short, usually only 3 to 4 feet in length, with a loop at one end and nothing at the other. You can make one out of a piece of $\frac{1}{4}$-inch rope cut to length and then simply tie a loop at one end of it. The loop end is attached to your belt, while the opposite end is fed

A check cord, or long line, offers more range of motion than a leash does while still affording you some control and the ability to issue corrections.

through the ring of your dog's collar and then grasped in your left hand (right hand if the dog is being trained on your right side) so that you can use the cord like a leash to control the dog. To release the dog, all you need to do is let go of the cord; as the dog runs off, the cord easily slips through the collar ring and the dog is free.

LAUNCHERS AND WINGERS

A dummy launcher is a special tool that uses a powder charge (usually a 22-caliber blank cartridge) to propel a dummy farther than you can by hand. It works well for increasing the distance that a pup will have to go to make a retrieve, but it has its drawbacks as well.

I do not consider the dummy launcher useful for much more than giving a dog a few long marks when there is no one available to help you. The launcher is typically used with the dog at heel, so it is best used only after the dog has been taught to be steady at the line and is making long retrieves. Because the dog is normally at your side when the launcher is fired, it gives a rather unusual mark for the dog in that the bumper is coming from the same location as the dog and sailing directly away from him. Therefore, the dog does not get a good look at the arc of the bumper and can easily mismark the fall. One thing that you can do with the launcher, which makes its use more fun and a bit more realistic, is to hup the dog as he is running around a field and then, with his focus on you, launch a bumper in a somewhat random direction. This gives the dog a variety of angles, distances, cover elements, and a host of other factors to deal with in making the retrieve, all of which can be a boon to his education. The problem is that you really have to make sure that your dog is very steady and controlled before you proceed with this technique.

A winger is a stationary device that launches a bumper or bird and can be outfitted with a remote control. Wingers tend to be used more often in retriever training than spaniel training, but that is quickly changing. Although not cheap, wingers are valuable to a person training alone. A winger does not throw bumpers or birds particularly far, but it does throw them in a way that is more realistic and helps the dog mark the object well. Having two or three wingers allows you to set up retrieving scenarios that realistically mimic the downing of multiple birds.

The problem with the winger is that it can launch only once and then it has to be reset. So although it is good to have a piece of equipment that will throw a nice mark from a distance, walking 100 yards or so every time your pup makes a retrieve just to reset the equipment can get a bit old quite quickly. Still, I think that having two or three wingers available for setting up a variety of marks can be valuable, especially with water marks, although they are not at all necessary for accomplishing your intended task.

A better tool than either the dummy launcher or winger for the individual trainer is a Bumper Boy launcher. Although you will be shelling out a good amount of change for this product, you will be able to consistently launch specially designed bumpers to a repeatable mark over and over again. The number of bumpers that can be launched, and therefore the number of marks you can give your dog, is limited primarily to the amount of money you want to spend.

Working on Retrieving

Because retrieving is the basic necessity in training your dog for the field, I prefer to begin working on it before moving on to quartering or field work. Just be sure to continue your pup's exposure to changing cover conditions, and encourage him to get out ahead of you as you

wander about the meadows and woodlots, or your efforts at instilling retrieving skills may cause him to be a bit "sticky," that is, unwilling to leave your side. You can actually work on quartering and retrieving simultaneously, but you will find that you have fewer problems getting through the early

A started dog is also skilled at land retrieves, delivering the bird to hand.

The thrower chooses an area without cover and uses a bumper that will be visible to the dog in the air and on the ground.

quartering work if you have a fairly solid retrieve established first. Putting off your quartering work for a couple of weeks while you take the time to establish a good retrieve will be worth the delay.

MARKED RETRIEVES

When referring to a marked retrieve, I am writing about when your pup sees the object that he is to retrieve as it is in the air and falling to the ground or water. The dog is to mark (identify the location of) the object and go directly to it to pick up and retrieve, preferably to hand. A dog cannot mark what he does not or cannot see, so be aware of whether your dog has actually seen the

bumper. If your pup was distracted by a songbird and looked away just as a bumper was thrown, he could not have marked it. Therefore, you should not send the dog to retrieve, because he cannot retrieve something he did not mark.

The early retrieves you throw for your pup are marked retrieves, but up to this point you have done a lot of informal play retrieves and demanded little more from your pup than his simply bringing the bumper or bird to you. The day has now arrived when you will begin to demand more from him to refine his retrieving skills.

While undergoing this training, a pup will progress from short retrieves on mowed ground to long retrieves in cover and from single to multiple marks. Your pup will also learn to be steady at your side or at the line (the point at which the dog is positioned and placed while waiting for and watching his marks thrown), and that will go a long way toward helping you train your pup to be steady to wing and shot. Refinement begins with regular retrieving sessions incorporated into the pup's training regimen. Having such sessions three to five days a week, two to three times each day, will be the key to moving your pup along at a reasonable pace.

Marked retrieve training necessitates your having an assistant; without one, you will make only moderate progress at best. When first transitioning to this more formal training, it is usually better to introduce your pup to your assistant in a place where the pup is comfortable and quite apt to retrieve anything thrown. Be sure that you are working on mowed ground or in very light cover. When the pup is comfortable with the assistant, take the pup to the spot from which he will retrieve—the line—and have him face in the direction of your assistant as he sits at your left side. Attach your belt loop to the dog as described earlier, and use it only for light control; you will not start to steady your pup quite yet. At a distance of no more than 10 to 20 yards, have the assistant get the pup's attention by calling "Pup, pup, pup" (not the pup's name) and, as the pup looks at the source of the sound, signal your assistant to throw a white bumper about 20 yards out and in a high arc. The color and the high arc of the bumper make it easy for the pup to see it in the air and on the ground, which will improve his chances of making the retrieve. Release your dog as the bumper is thrown by saying his name or whatever command you will use to tell him to retrieve. When he picks up the bumper, give your come whistle and have him bring the bumper to you.

Pups, being pups, will do any number of things once they have the bumper. One of the more common antics is to grab the bumper and stand there looking around or to begin playing with it. If this happens, call the pup again and begin to clap your hands as you run away from him. This will often draw him to you, where you can praise and reward him for a job well done. If this scenario seems to be playing out more often than not, then attach a long line to the pup and use it to correct him for not coming back to you properly. Another little trick the young dog often tries is to run to the assistant either on his way to the bumper or on his way back. If this happens, have your assistant stand perfectly still and ignore the dog. He should not make eye contact with or talk to the pup. Once the pup realizes that he is going to be ignored, he will often follow through with his mission. If not, you can use either of the tricks mentioned earlier to get him back to you.

STRETCHING HIM OUT

As with most retrieving sessions, have the pup do no more than four to six retrieves like this, and then move on to other things. At the next training session, do another series of four to six such retrieves until the pup is frequently going directly to the bumper and retrieving it to you without hesitation. Now it is time to increase the distance the pup will have to go to make a retrieve. To do this, you will want a mowed area that is about 100 yards long. Establish the line and have your assistant set up 20 yards straight out from the line and about 10 or 15 yards to either side of it. He will

park himself in that location with at least six and as many as twelve white bumpers; for our purposes, we will assume twelve bumpers. Bring your dog to the line, put him on a sit, and hook him up to your belt cord. When you are ready, signal for the assistant to get the pup's attention and throw the mark. Release the pup as the mark is thrown, and follow the same scenario as before. Have the pup make three retrieves from this line.

As the pup is running to the bumper on the third retrieve, move back another 20 yards so you are now 40 yards from where the mark will be thrown, and have the pup make three retrieves from this line. Again, as the pup is going out to make his third retrieve, move back another 20 yards—you are now 60 yards from the mark—and repeat this process until you have moved out to around 80 yards and have used all of the bumpers. This will be plenty of retrieves for this session.

Take a minute here to realize what you have been able to accomplish. You have just taken the pup from a short retrieve of 20 yards and quadrupled it to 80 yards. However, this does not mean that your pup is ready to do nothing but 80-yard retrieves. It simply means that you have extended his range and introduced him to longer

Steady by your side is where you want your spaniel to be before going out for a retrieve.

marks. Follow this same scenario for the next several sessions. Then begin to make your shortest marks, the first ones done in the series, start at 40 yards, and following the same technique, stretch the pup out to where he makes regular 100-yard marks. Once he is there, you can begin to work on having him be steady at the line.

STEADY AT THE LINE

Up until now, your belt cord has been used simply to keep the pup from getting too out of control as you ready for the bumper to be thrown. You are now to a point at which you will use it to let your pup know that leaving before being given the command to retrieve is no longer allowed.

Set up your training session as you normally do, beginning at a distance of 20 yards. With your pup in the heel position (sitting at your left side), run your belt cord through the ring of his collar, grab the end of it firmly with your left hand, and make certain that the cord is loose. By the way, be sure you are wearing gloves. Signal for the bumper to be thrown, and maintain a good grip on the cord as the bumper is thrown. Your pup is likely to break in anticipation of making the retrieve. When he does, he will take up all the slack in the cord; when that happens, you

want to give a good jerk backward and tell him "no—heel," meaning "sit at my side."

If he is a driven pup, you may have to settle him down a bit before being able to send him on the retrieve. Set him back up at your side, and try to have him focus on the bumper that was tossed. If you believe he is focused in on it, then send him as you normally would. If he has lost focus, have your assistant pick up the bumper and then throw another. Repeat this process for the next retrieve and every retrieve after it until your pup is reasonably steady at the line. It is only after the pup has made dozens of retrieves and been steady from a variety of distances, with the belt cord attached, that you should attempt to start testing his steadiness without the cord.

From this point onward, your dog has to understand that you expect steadiness at all times. What do you do if the pup should break (not remain steady)? For one, try to prevent the retrieve. If the assistant can get to the bumper before the pup does, then have him go and pick up the bumper. Regardless, though, you need to call your pup back right away with the "no—heel" command. I find that the well-trained pup will usually respond to this command

Working in cover adds difficulty to the retrieve, as the bumper or bird will not be readily visible to your dog.

RETRIEVING IN COVER

It may not seem as if there should be much difference between retrieving in cover and retrieving on bare ground, but there is a lot of difference. Bare ground makes it easy for the pup to find the bumper or bird even if he has momentarily lost his focus on it. Cover makes it likely that the pup is going to have to search for the bumper before he can actually make the retrieve, and a loss of focus may mean not getting the bumper at all. For this reason, you want the pup to be able to concentrate on the bumper as it is thrown or on the bird as it falls to the ground after being shot. That concentration makes it more likely that the dog will properly mark the location and not need to rely so much on sight as on memory. This is why you should not do much retrieving, other than short and simple play retrieves, in cover prior to getting the pup steady at the line.

I like to transition pups to retrieving in cover over the course of a few days and by gradually increasing the amount of cover in which they are working. You should always keep a few things in mind when working the retrieve drills in cover. First, the size of your pup will determine the distance at which he can mark well. The average-size English Springer is going to have a

quite quickly; if he doesn't and you have the wherewithal to do so, chase him down, grab him, and take him back to the line, giving him a forceful "no—heel" as you put him back in his place. Let him understand that breaking is simply not permissible. If you can't prevent him from getting the bumper before you can correct him for breaking, then simply let him bring the bumper back to you; however, do not praise in any manner. Take him back to the line and set up for another retrieve, but be prepared to be able to control him with your belt cord so that he does not try this again.

greater field of view than will the average-size Sussex simply because the Springer's head will be a good foot or more higher off the ground. This means that a Springer will be able to mark bumpers and birds better at a greater distance than will the smaller Sussex.

Next, the contour of the terrain can affect a dog's ability to properly mark a fall. In the early days of training, you want to train for retrieving on fairly level ground. As the pup progresses, you will introduce him to hills, valleys, ditches, creeks, and a slew of other elements that can affect his ability to quickly locate the mark, but not until he is accustomed to cover.

Finally, as with most new elements introduced in training, you should transition to cover rather than jumping right into the middle of it. That means working in light cover first and slowly expanding to retrieves in heavy cover. If you take your puppy immediately from a mowed field to one that consists of practically impenetrable knee-high grasses, you are setting him up for failure and setting your training back a peg or two. Start with cover that is about a foot high and easily penetrated by your pup, then move to something that is still easily penetrated but a bit taller, with a few patches of heavy cover now and then, and finally move to retrieves in or through stands of cover such as cattails, rose hedges, and the like.

Your job as trainer is to help your dog meet with success more often than with failure. To do that when working retrieves in cover, you want to begin, as you did on the mowed ground, with short retrieves that are gradually lengthened. This makes it more likely that the pup will find the bumper in quick order. As you lengthen the retrieves, it becomes more and more difficult for the pup to peg his mark, which means that he goes directly to and practically steps on the mark. What will often happen is that the pup will get to the area of the fall and then have to hunt around for the bumper or bird. If it takes him too long to find the mark, he may quit and return without the retrieve. So to help him be successful and avoid such a situation, you can scatter a number of bumpers around a specific area that will be used as the landing zone for the thrown marks. That way, when the pup arrives in the zone, he will find a bumper, even if it's not the one that was thrown, and return straight away with it. If you use this technique and find that the pup is playing too much with all of the scattered bumpers, then discontinue this little trick.

Spaniels are prized by many hunters for their versatility, being skilled on land and in water.

Another way to help the pup meet with success if he has failed to find the bumper is to have your assistant walk out to the bumper and encourage the pup into the area by calling "Pup, pup, pup." This will often draw the pup to the area, where he can sniff around and find his prize. Should this fail, the assistant can reach down and pick up the bumper, calling the pup over with a "Pup, pup, pup" and tossing the bumper straight up in the air when the pup is watching. The assistant should then stand perfectly still while the pup makes his retrieve. Avoid helping the dog out yourself, or he just may begin to wait for you to do so every time.

Moving into Water Retrieves

If your pup has not been introduced to water and is not freely swimming, you can stop right here and tackle that problem before moving on. Assuming, though, that your water introduction has been completed and your pup is eagerly swimming and making short play retrieves in the water, let's look at a few nuances regarding water retrieves. Because this is a book on training a flushing spaniel, I am not going to go as in depth into the water retrieve training techniques as I would if this were a book about training the nonslip retriever. If you will be using your pup as a waterfowl dog on more than an occasional basis, you should study the techniques for training a nonslip retriever found in any of the dozens of books on the subject.

By the time you take your pup to water with the purpose of working on formalized water retrieve training, he should be steady at the line, making reliable retrieves out to a distance of 100 yards on mowed ground, and responsive to whistle and voice commands. Your early training should be done on wide bodies of water that do not lend themselves to bank running (where a dog will run down or around the shore to get closer to the bumper or bird before going into the water). Too many spaniel owners dismiss bank running as a nonissue, and some even think of it as something to be proud of rather than as an issue to address. In fact, bank running can cause an inappropriate disturbance of the area around the shore and poor marks.

Still using an assistant here, you will set up a line just as you did for the marked retrieves on land. Start your water retrieves near the water's edge to help prevent the pup from wanting to run the bank and to reduce any tendency toward balking at entering the water. If you can find a narrow point of land that juts out into a large pond or lake, you will have found the ideal spot to prevent bank running. I have also started some pups out by establishing the line a short distance out in the water to avoid both a poor entry and bank running.

Over time, you will make your line farther and farther from shore. Your early retrieves should be short and gradually lengthened to between 80 and 100 yards. Do not go too fast with lengthening the retrieves because it is not very easy to correct for or to recover from a refused retrieve when you are working on the water.

The first common problem you will likely encounter is the pup's

desire to drop the bumper or bird along the shore before bringing it to you. This can be addressed in a couple of ways, the first one being that you simply meet him when he reaches the shore and grab the bumper before he drops it. As time goes on, you move farther and farther from the shoreline, doing so in small increments. The idea is to have the dog come to understand through habit that a bird retrieved from the water is to be brought to you and not dropped on the shore first. This is my preferred way of dealing with the problem, but you can also try getting excited as the pup reaches the water's edge and running away from the pup as you excitedly encourage him to follow. This does not always work, but if it does, you should continue to draw the pup toward you until he is close enough for you to reach down and take the bumper.

Another problem that can develop is that a pup will take the bird or bumper and run off with it or play with it a short distance out in the water. If this happens, you need to go back to working your pup on leash and making very short retrieves into the water. The use of a flexible leash (a retractable long line available at most pet stores) can work well for you here. The longest retrieve you will get using a flexible leash is a bit shy of 10 yards, but that should not matter. What you want to do here is to let the pup know that you will not tolerate any games and that he is to come to you no matter what. Normally, if you do not have such delivery problems with your land retrieves, you will not have any with your water retrieves either, but you need to be prepared in advance to nip this problem in the bud quickly in case it occurs.

DECOYS

Once your pup is making water retrieves of 60 to 80 yards, is steady at the line, and is bringing the bird to you after returning, you can begin to increase the difficulty of his water work. I first like to introduce a few decoys on the water to serve as a distraction to the dog and to get him learning to ignore distractions and concentrate on the bumper or bird. This is good for any dog, whether he will be used for duck hunting or not. Decoys are brought into the equation on land first by placing a couple of decoys in the yard or field and having the pup heel through and around them. Keep his attention on you as he heels, and if he goes to sniff or investigate the decoy, give him a quick leash correction and the command "no, leave it" to tell him to leave the decoys alone.

Once you can reliably heel him through decoys without his being distracted by them, you can begin to give him some retrieves near the decoys, but not in or through them quite yet. Have a few training sessions with the decoys about 5 yards or so off to one side of where the bumper will be falling. If your pup runs off to check the decoys, give him a firm "no, leave it." If he does not listen to you, then go get him and have a talk about how the decoys are off limits. After he is making reliable retrieves with the decoys off to one side, give him some retrieves from the middle of them. Spread half a dozen decoys out in a large area, leaving 4 to 6 feet between each, and have the bumper thrown into the middle of this grouping. Send your pup and expect him to retrieve properly as he ignores the decoys. When he is doing this reliably, you can begin to give him retrieves through the decoys, which requires that you have the bumper thrown over and behind the spread of decoys so that he has to run through the decoys to get the bumper. As always, do not tolerate any tendency toward sniffing or otherwise investigating any of the decoys.

If your dog will reliably ignore decoys on land, he is likely to do so on the water, but here you will have to follow a similar procedure to what you did on land by first giving him retrieves to the side, then in the midst of, and finally through the decoy spread.

WATER COVER

At this point, you can begin to work your dog into and through cover when making water retrieves. As always, begin with light cover and work your way up to the heavy stuff. First introduce cover by having a bumper tossed just inside the edge of cover on the far side of the water. This gives the dog the security of open water and has him needing only to stick his nose into the cover for a quick moment. As training progresses, the bumper is thrown deeper and deeper into cover so that the dog must learn to navigate into and out of it. Finally, the bumper is thrown on the opposite side of a patch of cover so that the dog learns to navigate all the way through the cover and to return back through it as well.

Once the dog has completed this process with cover opposite the near shore, begin to establish lines in front of cover that is against the near shoreline. Here the dog has to learn to plow through the cover to get to open water and find the mark. Finally, look for areas where you can put all of these elements

You can progress to working in water cover after your dog is comfortable with basic water retrieves.

together and work your dog extensively in cover on the water. When the day comes that you drop a nice rooster pheasant breaking out of a cattail patch in the middle of a 2-acre pothole choked by reeds, you will be awfully glad that you did all of this training.

Quartering the Field

One of the greatest reasons for having a dog as a hunting companion is to take advantage of his superior scenting ability. With an olfactory system that is reportedly

1,000 times greater than that of humans, a spaniel can detect bird scent from dozens of yards away and tell whether that scent was left there yesterday or belongs to a cagey rooster trying to escape the predators that just entered his territory. Obviously, you want to put this attribute to good use while in the field. To do that, you want the dog to check for birds within a fairly defined area in front of you as you are moving through a field or a woodlot. This is defined as quartering a field, and although some spaniels seem to have a natural propensity for doing this, it is a good idea to establish a quartering pattern with your dog or at least the ability to control his natural pattern, should he have one. In the end, what you want is a spaniel that will quarter a field approximately 15 to 25 yards in front of you and about the same distance to either side because this puts a flushed bird well within gun range.

As you have already established the fundamentals with your pup, he is well prepared for this training, but let's recap here for a minute before we go any further. You do not want to start this training unless you are certain that your pup will come when called. Because birds will often be used in the training process, you must have your pup

retrieving well. Although some quartering training can be done on bare ground, it is helpful to have the pup accustomed to cover when this work begins. As you proceed through this training process, your dog will be learning a new whistle command that helps you direct him through the field, so be sure to always have your whistles with you. In fact, once your dog has come to understand any of the whistle commands, you should always have your whistles readily available during training sessions.

There are two common methods used to establish a quartering pattern in a spaniel—one for the individual who must train on his own, and the other for the hunter who is training with at least two helpers. Since most trainers are more likely to be training on their own, we will discuss that process first and then move on to look at how a couple of helpers can be added to the process.

Just You and Your Pup

In choosing a training location for the quartering drills, seek out an area of light (grass about 9 inches or so high) to medium (grass between 12 inches and 18 inches high) cover that is not very dense. The pup should be able to easily penetrate the cover and locate birds but should not be able to spy a planted bird from more than a few feet away. If you cannot find anything but mowed grounds, then make do with what you have, although this is not the ideal. The field should be roughly the size of a football field to provide you with enough room to work.

During the early weeks of training, you will want to work the puppy into the wind as much as possible. A head wind tends to have a dog work in close to the handler rather than farther out and away. The more often the pup is in close to you, the more likely it is that he will establish a close working style. If you were to work with the wind at your back or sharply coming in from the left or right, you would surely have a dog that would push out farther than preferred, and in time you would find your control of the dog waning. As your training progresses to a higher and higher level, you will be setting up training sessions that use tail and crossing wind patterns, but it is best to avoid those for right now.

Because you are aware of the wind direction and the field size, you can locate the proper starting point for your trek along one side of the field. It is recommended that you mark this starting point in some way to establish an easily found

reference point in the field. (A piece of survey tape attached to a branch or a bicycle flag inserted in the ground works well.) Once you have marked the spot, turn and face into the wind. Pick a point out across the field that will serve as an ending point for your venture, and then walk out and mark that point as well. Ideally, the distance between these two points should be about 100 yards, but a bit more or less is just fine. The path that is formed by drawing an imaginary line between these two marks will form the center of your overall path through the field.

You are almost ready to start the pup out, but first you need to follow a few more steps to be properly prepared. Make sure that you have a hunting vest that you can use to carry a few (three to four is plenty) dead birds with you in the field. Have your whistle handy and a long line of about 20 to 30 feet in length available if you need it. Be sure to put a bottle of water in your vest to keep your dog hydrated while you are training.

Before getting the pup out, walk to your starting point, and toss a dead bird about 10 yards to the right and 5 to 10 yards down the field. (It really does not matter on which side you place the bird; I am just using the right side for the purposes of this discussion. In fact, you want to vary the sides so that your dog does not begin to anticipate what is coming next.) Next, toss a second bird about 10 yards to the left and about 5 to 10 yards farther down the field from where you tossed the bird on the right.

Should you not have access to dead birds, it is possible to use retrieving bumpers in place of birds. In this case, I like to attach bird wings to the bumpers so that the dog can pick up on the bird scent and does not need to rely on his sight to locate the bumpers. You want the pup to learn to use his nose more than his eyes when quartering a field, or you might end up with a pointing, rather than a flushing, spaniel.

OK, now go get your pup. When you bring him to the starting point, you will face down the field, toward the ending point marker, but your pup is going to be placed on a hup immediately in front of and facing you. You want to avoid having the pup face down the field because this could cause him to race straight away from you rather than to one side or the other. With the pup's concentration focused on you, he is less apt to be drawn off in a wrong direction.

You are going to cast—meaning send—your dog to the right, toward the bird that you placed there earlier. To do this, you will tell him "get on" and extend your right arm out as you begin to walk toward the bird. Most pups tend to want to walk out in front of you, so your movement toward the bird should put the pup a little ahead of you and able to come across that dead bird in short order. Once he does, if the foundation work has been done properly, he will pick up the bird and bring it right to you; when he does, give him a lot of praise for having found and retrieved a bird.

Now, give him the *get on* command again, but this time extend your left arm and head to the other side of your center line toward the bird you threw there. Continue to work the dog toward the bird on the left, and when he finds and retrieves it, lavish him with praise again. After taking the bird from the pup, cast him to the right just as you did before, and move toward the right side of your center line; walk a few yards past the center line, and then give him two pips (*tweet-tweet*) on the whistle along with the left arm signal, and begin walking toward the left. Your pup will likely turn and follow you, trying to get out ahead of you where all the birds are.

Keep walking to the left for several yards, and as your pup is moving out ahead and not watching you, toss a bird in on the right side of the center line (this is known as "rolling a bird behind the dog") about 10 yards out and 5 to 10 yards down the field. Give the *tweet-tweet* signal, and motion with your right arm that you are changing direction again. Walk your dog to that bird until he finds it, and praise when he does. Now give the *get on* command and head to your left until you are a few yards to the left of the center line, then switch direction with a *tweet-tweet* and a right hand signal. Once again, continue walking to the right as you toss a bird to the left, but make sure your pup does not see it thrown. Once the bird is in place, give the whistle and hand signals to turn the pup and head him off in the direction of the bird, praising him when he has found and brought you his latest discovery. Continue to follow this crisscrossing pattern until you have reached the end of the course or until the pup has gotten five to six finds.

Once you have reached the end of the field, leash your pup and walk him back to a place where he can rest for a short while. After a period of rest, run this whole scenario again, and then stop for the day. I find that two good runs per training session are sufficient to

Marking the course you will take through a training field helps keep you facing the wind and on a predetermined path. Your young pup will benefit from such effort.

establish, improve, and maintain a good quartering pattern. Obviously, if you can do the quartering drill every day, your dog is going to be well trained sooner rather than later; practically speaking, however, you are not likely to have that much opportunity to train. If at all possible, though, do your best to get in three such sessions every week with no more than three days between sessions.

If your pup is one of those that does not want to follow you and make those turns, then you will need to resort to the use of a long line. Attach a long line to the pup and allow him to drag it through the field as you are working with him. When you want the pup to turn, give your whistle signal and then grab the long line and give a quick pull on the cord, walking in whatever direction you want him to go. That should be enough to get him to come along with you; if not, continue to give little jerks on the cord and further guide him. Eventually, the pup will catch on, and you will be able to dispense with the check cord.

As Pup Progresses

If you are working on the quartering drill a minimum of three sessions per week, you will soon find the pup crisscrossing the field on his own rather than needing constant guidance from you. As this starts to occur, you want to reduce the amount of movement you make to either side of the center line, eventually extinguishing it altogether. However, you will want to keep on using your whistle and arm signals every time the pup changes direction, be it on his own or with your urging.

You will also continue to use planted and rolled-in birds as a way of enticing the dog to continue to search the field for birds. Early on in the training, you want the pup to be getting a lot of birds in fairly quick succession as a means of keeping his interest piqued. However, the time will come when you need to start giving the dog a taste of reality and letting him know that a bird is not always going to be found on every cast, or even every few casts, for that matter. When this time arrives, you have a couple of options. If you prefer using preplanted birds to those that are rolled in, you can simply spread them farther apart in the field. For example, you could place your first bird just 5 yards down the field and 15 yards to your left, followed by the next bird that is another 15 yards down the field and 20 yards to the right, and the third bird that is 40 yards down the field and 10 yards to the left of the center line, and so forth. This pattern starts the pup out with a quick find or two, keeping his interest up while letting him come to understand that birds may not always be found so readily.

Another technique is to roll all the pup's birds in behind him when you feel it is necessary. I use this technique more with dogs that have progressed further along in their training program than with beginners, but it can be used at any time. Simply keep an eye on your dog's enthusiasm, and if you see it waning and see him growing a bit frustrated over not finding birds, roll a bird in behind him and let him suddenly reap the benefits of a job well done. This is a great time for using a taped-wing pigeon or chukar, too. These birds will not be lying motionless on the ground when the dog approaches; instead, their running or attempting to fly will turn on the pup's prey drive and really spark his interest in finding another bird just like the last. You will see a definite difference between the pup's earlier quartering work and that which is done following his ability to get a taped-wing bird.

Rolled-in birds can be placed anywhere along the course you are running, including directly in front of you. However, if you put too many birds immediately in front of you when the dog is in the first few months of training on this exercise, you may cause him to work too close to you. Such a dog fails to "get on" much to either side of you because he comes to understand that the birds are not "out there" but are directly in front of you, so why should he work farther away? Rolling birds in close to you can work to your benefit when you have a dog that pushes out too far in front of you and needs to be drawn back in. After rolling a few birds in

just a couple of yards in front of you, the dog soon starts to work closer.

A HELPFUL TECHNIQUE

I have described a way in which you can train your dog to quarter a field all on your own, but there is another way. Some feel this is the best way, and it may very well be; however, it is not always a convenient way for the average trainer to tackle this task. Still, you need to

Give your dog opportunities to succeed so that he'll always be enthusiastic in the field.

know about this technique so that you can utilize it should you have the opportunity. If you are lucky enough to train with a local spaniel club, the odds are that this is the way you will train. This quick overview will give you a bit of insight into what will transpire. If you have some friends to help you train, regardless of whether or not you belong to a spaniel club, you may find that this technique will move things along a little faster.

Everything that was described in the earlier quartering technique will hold true for this one as well, with a couple of major exceptions. Instead of just you and your pup in the field, you will have two helpers to handle the birds for you. One of these helpers will be situated about 10 to 15 yards to your right, and the other will be the same distance to your left. I will refer to these people as your left and right gunners, because that is exactly what they are simulating—a couple of fellow hunters (gunners) out with you for a day of hunting.

When you enter the field, you will take the dog to the starting point and have him face you. The gunners, if not already there, will position themselves appropriately. Each will be carrying two birds, one in his game vest and the other in his hand. No birds will be preplanted in the field. As you move, so will the gunners. That means that if you stop, they stop, and if you move forward, they move forward. However, in the beginning, you will stand still, making no forward movement at all.

It is time to cast your pup off. Before you do, have the left gunner start talking in an excited voice to the pup and shaking the dead bird in his hand, low toward the ground to draw the pup's attention. Have a hold of the pup's collar so that he does not bolt before you can cast him off; wait for him to get excited about all the commotion. When you think the pup is sufficiently excited, cast him off with the *get on* command and a hand signal. As the pup runs and gets near the gunner, have the gunner lift the bird up and tuck it under his arm so the pup cannot see it as easily. Have this gunner go silent, and then have the right gunner begin to talk excitedly and shake his bird to draw the pup's attention. As the pup turns to run to the right gunner, give a *tweet-tweet* on your whistle and encourage your pup toward him. When the pup gets to the right gunner, have the left gunner draw the pup back to him. Again, as the pup turns, give him the whistle and hand signals.

As your pup is running back toward the left gunner, have the right gunner toss his dead bird just a couple of yards directly in front of himself. Once the dog gets to the left gunner, have this gunner go silent and the right gunner begin to draw the pup back over. Give your whistle and hand signal as the pup turns to head to the right. This time when he gets to that gunner, he should scent the bird, as you are working with the wind in your face, and it will carry the scent directly to the dog. Your dog will likely locate and retrieve the bird to you, so give him lots of praise when he does. Now repeat this process, making sure that your dog gets his next bird on the opposite side of where he got his first bird.

After two birds are given on each side, stop the session and go do something else. Come back a short while later, and repeat what you did here one more time. Notice that you are not walking down the field quite yet. In fact, I recommend that you complete this regimen during three separate training sessions before beginning to move down the field.

When it comes time to begin moving the dog down the field, he will already have a pretty good idea that what he is supposed to do is to work back and forth from one side of the field to the other. However, you still need to have the gunners following the steps (talking to the dog and shaking the birds) outlined earlier until the dog gets to the point where he begins to turn back in the opposite direction before any signaling or encouragement occurs. Once that happens, slowly reduce the amount of encouragement given until you extinguish it altogether, and then use it only when necessary.

Your first attempt at moving the pup down the field as he quarters from side to side begins exactly as the last steps were outlined. However, after the dog has made two complete passes (a complete pass occurs when the pup has crisscrossed the field and passed in front of the handler twice) and gotten a bird on each side of your center line, you begin to move forward after casting the dog off to whatever side you choose.

Let the gunners entice the pup back and forth through the field until he has made two passes without being given a bird. Then have the gunner that is farthest from the pup roll in a bird, making sure that the pup does not see the bird go down. As before, have the gunner go silent and wait for the pup to locate and retrieve the bird. Now set your dog up in front of you as you have been doing, and cast him to the side opposite of where he got the bird. Again, have him make a couple of passes, and then have the other gunner roll in his bird. After the pup has found and retrieved the bird, you will give him one more pass and a bird on the opposite side of his last one. Once the bird is in your hands, release your dog and let him relax. Wait a while and then repeat these steps again before calling it a day.

As the pup progresses in his training, you will need to eliminate or alter a few of the steps in this training scenario. First, you will extinguish the initial passes back and forth without moving. Next, you will begin to expand on the number of passes made before the pup gets a bird; however, I rarely allow even the most advanced dog to go for more than four or five passes without a bird. Remember to incorporate a few taped-wing birds from time to time and, as the pup reaches the completion of this task, to put some flyers out there for him to flush. Finally, you will eliminate the gunners' shaking the birds and talking to the pup. Exactly when all of this occurs is really determined by the progress of each individual pup, so it is impossible to tell you when that time will come. However, if you think that you might be there, then give it a go and eliminate whatever it is you are thinking of doing away with. If your pup is not ready, you will know it in short order by the poor quality of his work. In that case,

just take a step back and reintroduce what you eliminated for a while longer.

I think that there are a couple of advantages to training in this manner. For one, it allows you to be totally focused on your pup, not having to worry about tossing in birds or other issues. Another advantage is that it establishes a crisscrossing pattern and at the same time teaches the dog to work between two gunners. This becomes invaluable if you should decide to participate in spaniel hunt tests or hunt with others. Furthermore, it gives you the ability to more easily draw the dog out into an ever-wider quartering pattern with greater ease than can be accomplished when training on your own. All in all, this method has more advantages than disadvantages and should become a part of every pup's training program if at all possible.

Taking the Shot

Every new gundog owner cannot seem to wait for the day when a bird that his pup flushed will be shot and subsequently retrieved by the dog. It seems to be a mark of maturity or a rite of passage from puppyhood to gundog, telling the owner that his dreams will one day be fulfilled. Pushing the arrival of that day on an accelerated time frame is not wise, but if you have followed the suggested regimen outlined here and you have assessed your pup's progress with an unbiased eye (which is admittedly hard to do), you should know when the time is right.

Some owners, usually serious hunt test participants or field trialers, will tell you not to shoot over your pup until you have him steady to wing and shot. I am not inclined to argue with that philosophy one bit! However, in looking at it from a practical perspective, I know that no matter how many times the average spaniel owner is told to wait until the dog is steady, he usually will not do it. Such a person is more inclined to shoot over his dog sooner rather than later, not worrying about the consequences; those can be dealt with later. With that in mind, let's forge ahead, although if you are inclined to wait until your pup has been steadied to wing and shot, return to this text and follow this process at that point.

Do not shoot over your pup until he has developed the following characteristics:

- is obedient to both verbal and whistle commands, especially the *come* command
- routinely quarters a field in search of game, responding well to your direction

Have a firm grip on the bird when shaking it for the pup, and keep the wings out so that the bird is easier for the pup to see.

- retrieves a dead bird to hand
- has been accustomed to gunfire using the steps outlined earlier and shows no concern about gunshots

If your dog has shown you that he has developed to this point in his training, then begin to shoot live birds for him from time to time.

It is at this point, when shooting over your dog, that you really need to enlist the help of a couple of assistants to be your gunners. These people will be there to concentrate on shooting the bird while you concentrate on controlling and

If your dog is very quick on the chase, you'll have to wait until there is sufficient distance between dog and bird before a shot is taken.

training your pup. The only thing that will change in your quartering drill here is that instead of pre-planting or rolling in a taped-wing or dead bird, you will be using flyers (birds that can fly away when flushed). Since rolling in a flyer is a bit of a skill and you want this to go off as smoothly as possible, I recommend that your first few sessions with shot flyers be done using pre-planted birds (birds that are planted and then shot, as opposed to birds that are allowed to fly away without being shot). I also suggest that you first give your pup his standard quartering exercise using only dead or taped-wing birds. Then in your second run of the exercise, put down one or two flyers for the pup to flush and your gunners to shoot. In fact, there is rarely a time when you need

to put down more than two or three flyers to maintain the pup's learned ability. Even dogs well past their prime and old hands at field work only need an occasional flyer to keep their skills honed, as dead and taped-wing birds are sufficient tools.

Be sure to have your gunners shoot only if the bird is well clear of the dog; they are not to shoot if you yell "no bird!" "No bird!" is your signal to the gunners that they are not to shoot under any circumstance. Why would you yell "no bird"? Usually because the pup is too close as he gives chase, and the bird is not flying high enough to put a sufficient distance between the bird and the dog to allow for a safe shot. In most cases, though, the bird will get airborne quickly enough to allow for a safe shot; when that happens, your dog is going to be on the move.

Eventually, you will train your pup to hup when the bird is flushed or a gun goes off, but for now this is not your area of concern. Right now you want to focus on having the dog locate and retrieve the shot bird. If you have truly done your early fundamental training, this will not be a problem. If the gunners miss this bird, however, there may be a problem. Should the gunners miss and should the dog have a good fix on the bird, he will likely give chase for a good distance across the field. Again, if you have trained the fundamentals well and trained your pup to come under all manner of distraction, you should be able to get him back to you in short order. If he does not return promptly, locate him and let him know that failing to come when called is a serious offense worthy of a good reprimand.

From this point on, your dog will gain more and more experience at finding, flushing, and retrieving shot flyers during regular training sessions. This experience will prove invaluable to your dog's ability to handle wild birds while afield and will certainly prove to be the core element needed to consistently fill your game bag.

Fieldwork is vigorous exercise; proper hydration for your dog is essential.

Keeping Your Dog Hydrated

Remember to keep your dog hydrated while in the field. In all the excitement of training a young pup and trying to concentrate on the many different nuances of training, this is easy to forget. My suggestion is that you offer the pup a drink after every other bird that he finds. If he turns down water, then either he does not need any or he is dangerously dehydrated. Talk to your veterinarian and learn how to tell the difference.

The best watering system for a dog in the field is a sport bottle full of cool water. Dogs quickly learn to drink from the flowing stream of water, and the bottles are easily carried in your vest. I start pups drinking from such a bottle when they are as young as eight weeks old. It takes no time at all for them to become accustomed to drinking this way, and it can, literally, be a lifesaver. Understand too that a dehydrated dog has reduced scenting ability, which can affect his training and his ability to hunt. Bottom line—offer your pup plenty of water and do it often.

As you progress in your training, your dog will become comfortable and confident in different types of cover.

Moving On Up:
Intermediate Training

Once you've developed your spaniel into a started hunting dog, it's time to cultivate his talents further. The exercises and program in this chapter will help turn your dog into a prized hunting companion.

Steadying to Wing and Shot

In the world of spaniels, a dog that has trained to be steady to wing and shot—that is, to hup and make no further forward progress upon flushing a bird or hearing a gunshot—has either reached the pinnacle of his training or is awfully darn close. Still there are a lot of spaniel folk who believe training to this level is useless and claim that their breaking dogs are as good as or better than any dog that is steady. This is one of those arguments that will never end, and it seems useless to try to justify either position, but I am going to put in a few words here on behalf of steadying the dog.

First, an unsteady dog gives chase, and he usually chases for a pretty good distance. If you are out with your dog on a hunt across prairie grasslands and flush a nice rooster that

A steady dog is a more reliable worker and companion for the hunter.

fall. What will you do now with a bird down but not marked by your dog? Do you think you can still find the bird? A steady dog would have been sitting and able to get a better mark on that bird than would one racing to the fall.

These are just two of the scenarios that should lead any hunter to want a dog steady to wing and shot. There are many others, but these alone should be enough to spur you into wanting to teach your dog to be steady.

Before your dog is ready to begin this part of his training, you want to make sure that he is quartering well and has a solid flush—not necessarily a bold one but definitely a deliberate one. Furthermore, your pup needs to fully understand and reliably respond to the *hup* whistle during all manner of distractions. A dog that does not hup to the whistle is not going to learn this aspect of his education as easily as one that does. Of course, it was already mentioned that the steady-at-the-line training done for the pup's retrieving drills will move this training along quite rapidly. So if your realistic evaluation of the pup reveals that he is where he should be to start this process, feel free to begin. If not, take the time to have him bone up on the weak areas before forging ahead.

escapes your shot, just how many other birds do you think your dog will bust out of cover when he chases that rooster? How long do you think it will take to get your dog back as he flushes one bird and chases it, then comes across another bird and chases it, and then . . . get the picture? An unsteady dog can turn your wonderful day afield into a nightmare.

Now let's say you hit the bird that flushed, but when you hit it your dog was chasing and happened to be in a ditch, unable to see the

You are going to steady your dog to both wing and shot, but you will work first at steadying the dog to wing and slip in the gunshot later. Steadying to the gunshot will go faster once you have established steadiness to wing. Teaching your pup to be steady is not all that difficult, but it does take time and a lot of consistency. It requires you to get the pup out in the field, romping on his own but willing to respond to your direction when needed. You will need to have your game vest, whistles, and a white or white-black bumper.

GETTING STARTED ON STEADYING

Walk the pup along, letting him cover the field as you normally would; after a bit of time passes, get his attention and toss a bumper up high so that he can easily see it. This toss should be away from and behind you, not toward the dog. As you toss the bumper, blow your *hup* whistle; if pup does not hup right away, go and get him. Once you have him, take him back to the spot where he was supposed to hup and blow your whistle again. He will probably hup this time, but if he does not, make sure he does. Tell him "stay," if you must, and walk back to where you were when you commanded him to hup

the first time. Reinforce the *hup* by giving another whistle blast and tell him "stay." Praise him if he does, and correct him if he does not. Now go over to the bumper and pick it up. He has not earned a retrieve, so don't give him one. Put the bumper in your vest and release your dog.

At this point, the dog is likely to come running over in hopes that you will throw the bumper again. Ignore him; in fact, ignore him until he is back to working the field again. This may take a while, for the dog now knows that you have a bumper, and he probably knows that you are more likely to throw it for him if he is at your side. Resist this at all costs. Even if you can't get in another toss in this session, do not throw the bumper.

Once the pup is working the field again, repeat the sequence outlined above. Praise your pup if he hups right away, and then decide whether you will give him this retrieve. At this point in his training, you need to begin to let him understand that not all retrieves are his to make; by doing that, you will prevent his anticipation of being sent. A dog that anticipates his retrieves usually creeps forward and is not really steady. By changing the frequency with which you send him on his retrieves, you will teach him to wait for the command rather than to anticipate it. I usually send a dog on only one retrieve in four while I work on steadying him, and always in a different sequence.

When you begin to train your dog to be steady to wing, you will almost certainly see that he does not hup at all but runs toward the retrieve. As I said earlier, when this happens, you need to get the pup and correct him as previously described. Within a relatively short period of time, your pup will probably begin to hup, but just not immediately. That is to say that when the bumper is tossed and the whistle blown, he will continue to run for a short distance before stopping. Even though he has hupped, you still need to get him and take him back to where he was told to hup, following the aforementioned corrective measures. He must understand that he is to put his rear end down without delay.

Eventually, your dog will begin to anticipate the hup command when he sees the bumper in the air and go into a hup. Give him the whistle signal anyway, and praise him lavishly for doing what was expected. After this begins to be the norm, you can start to toss the bumper in different directions, which will make it more difficult for the dog to resist being steady. Start

first by tossing the bumper out in front of him; when that is successful, begin to toss it over the dog's head as he is moving through the field. If he chooses to not be steady, your corrective actions are always the same.

Once you can toss a bumper anywhere around the field and have him be steady, you can switch to tossing dead birds. Follow the same sequence of events by first tossing the bird high and behind you, then high and in front of the dog, and then high and over the dog's head. Once that has been accomplished and he has demonstrated that he is steady with a dead bird, you can begin to use taped-wing birds in the same way. The only caveat here is that you do not throw a taped-wing bird over the dog's head. Why? I simply don't like that much temptation, and in any case, taped-wing birds are not that easy to toss very far. When your dog is reliably steady to a tossed dead bird, you can consider moving on to steadying him to the gun.

Steadying your dog to the gun is a fairly easy process, in that all you do is introduce gunfire as the bird is thrown and before the *hup* whistle is given. Soon the dog hears the sound of the gun and anticipates that a *hup* command is coming next, which induces him to hup. Do not fire a gun every time there is a bird tossed, for you will not be shooting at every bird flushed in the field while hunting. Instead, mix things up a bit, firing a gunshot about once in every four tosses, as you do with the retrieves. Speaking of retrieves, do not let the dog retrieve every time there is a gunshot, or you will have him breaking at the sound of the gun.

MIXING IN FLYERS

Just because your dog is steady to thrown-in bumpers, thrown-in birds, and the occasional gunshot, do not think that he is steady to wing quite yet. You now need to start mixing flyers into the dog's quartering pattern so that he has the ability to learn that steadiness is required under all conditions, even in the face of a bird flushing in front of his nose and flying off.

During your quartering sessions, you will want to have a combination of flyers and taped-wings either preplanted or rolled in behind the dog. When you are ready to introduce flyaways (birds able to flush and purposely allowed to fly off), you should begin with a mix of one bird in four being a flyer. When using a mixture of taped-wing birds and flyers, you should distribute the flyers randomly in the field so the dog does not learn a set pattern. As the dog's steadiness improves, you can regularly increase the number of

A dog's first reaction to a flushed flyer is to give chase.

flyers until that is all you have in the field. Given the price of birds, you will be best off using pigeons for this phase of training, or you will quickly go broke.

If you are lucky or have done a very good job with your early steadiness drills, your pup will flush a flyaway and quickly hup on his own or with the help of the whistle command. (I always give the whistle command.) However, it is more likely that when your pup first flushes a flyaway, he will give chase; let him do so until you see him beginning to slow down. At that point, you will blow the hup whistle. He should pop right into a hup, at which time you will praise and call him to you. If he does not hup properly, go and correct him as you

Allow your dog to chase the bird before giving the hup command, and eventually the desire to chase will diminish.

did in the earlier training drills. Allowing him to give chase helps him understand that he is not going to be able to catch the flyaway, and waiting for him to slow down makes it more likely that he will respond to your *hup* command. Over the course of a few training sessions, you will see your dog become less and less willing to chase the birds, and you will start to give that *hup* command sooner into the chase. Soon the day will come when you hup the dog right as the bird is being flushed or

when the dog simply hups on his own without your command. When this has become a common reaction to a flushed bird, it is time to start shooting over the dog.

SHOOTING THE FLYERS

You are at the point at which your dog flushes a bird and hups to the flush, remaining there until he is sent on his way or called back in to you. It is time for you to start shooting some of these flyers. Your concentration really needs to be on your dog and not on trying to shoot a flushed bird, so it is best if you have your assistant gunners handy to do the shooting. Set up the training session as you normally would, and put three or four birds in the field. Start your quartering work and keep a watchful eye on your dog. When he flushes a bird, give him the *hup* whistle. If he hups—and only if he hups—have the gunners shoot the bird. Immediately give a second *hup* whistle just to reinforce what he is to be doing. Wait a few seconds, and then send the dog to make the retrieve. Remember, you want to wait a bit before sending the dog to avoid teaching him to creep.

Notice that you should not have the gunners shoot the bird unless your dog has responded to the *hup* command. A bird shot before the dog is steady will likely cause the dog to break or simply never think of being steady. Your dog has to learn that there will be no shot and no retrieve unless he hups quickly and properly.

As with all other retrieving work, you need to make certain that the dog does not begin to think that every downed bird is his to retrieve. An attitude such as that leads only to a dog that breaks at the fall in anticipation of having or getting to retrieve. Therefore, when you don't want him to retrieve, repeat the *hup* whistle when the bird is shot to reinforce the hup as you walk toward the bird. Pick the bird up and carry it back to where you were. Now toss the bird off in a direction away from where the shot bird fell, and have your dog retrieve it. Follow this system quite regularly to avoid the prospect of teaching the dog to break at the fall.

Retrieving Multiple Marks

I am always surprised at how many spaniel enthusiasts seem to be almost put off by the prospect of shooting a double and their dogs' having to retrieve one to boot. Even in the AKC spaniel hunt test, game doubles are taboo, and many exhibitors bristle at the suggestion that when there is a double flush, both birds should be shot and retrieved. Why? I have no idea. Certainly, when hunting, if I have the opportunity and good fortune to shoot a double, I will take it and I will expect my dog to retrieve both birds. Does this happen often? Absolutely not, at least not in the uplands, but when it does, I like knowing that the dog is prepared to handle it. With that in mind then, let's take some time to talk about training your dog to make multiple marked retrieves.

You do not want to start this work until the dog is working well on single marks, both on land and

Maintaining Steadiness

At this point, your dog has become steady to wing and shot. Like any athlete, he cannot maintain his abilities without regular practice, and that means having to take the time to occasionally give the dog shot birds throughout the year. If you plan to maintain your dog's working abilities, regularly planned quartering sessions with planted or rolled-in flyers will be a necessary part of his training program for years to come.

Use dummies that will be easily visible on grass to begin multiple-mark training.

in the water. I also do not recommend you do this until the quartering work is done, although I am not so concerned about having the dog steady to wing and shot prior to introducing multiple marks. You will need to go back to mowed ground as you start this new process, and an assistant is definitely needed for this training.

When you train a dog to properly mark and handle multiple retrieves, you are teaching him to use both his visual sense and his memory. It is the memory exercise that can become a problem for the dog, but it is a problem that will easily be overcome in time and by following a few simple steps. A dog's ability to remember marks requires repeated training sessions throughout his life

as a gundog. Once trained to do multiple marks, he will need to keep doing them on a regular basis.

In that multiple marks are nothing more than two separate retrieves, there will be very little difference between how you set up for this training sequence and how you set up previously for the single marked retrieves. A couple of cautions are in order, though. First, be sure to separate the two marks by a wide angle, even out to as much as 180 degrees, or you will risk having the dog switch bumpers. A switch occurs when the dog is heading for one particular mark and then decides to switch to the other mark. You want to prevent your dog from switching because it often leads to failure to complete the two retrieves, not to mention that it unnecessarily disturbs too much ground.

Next, now that you are throwing more than one bumper or bird and your dog has been doing a lot of quartering work, it will help if you work the dog with the wind at your back or with a crossing wind. This will help the dog take a straighter line and make him use his eyes (remember, he is marking this bird) more so than his nose. With a crossing wind, make sure that it is not blowing from the direction of your memory bird (the first bird thrown), or the wind may cause your dog to switch (more on that later). Furthermore, now that you are training multiple marks, you need to go back to basics, and that means starting with short retrieves on bare ground. You can make them longer retrieves as the dog progresses, but not for a while. If you happen to have two assistants who can throw marks for you, great; if not, one assistant will do.

Take your dog back to the mowed field and establish your retrieving line (the point from which you will send your dog). Have your two assistants spread out somewhere between 90 and 180 degrees apart and about 20 yards or so out from the line. Decide which assistant is going to throw the first mark (for our purposes, we will say it is the right-hand assistant), and turn your dog to face that mark. Nothing has changed here, so you will tell the dog to hup and have him sit at your left side. By this time, he should be steady at the line and not need the belt cord attached, but for reasons you will soon understand, attach it anyway. Signal your assistant to throw the mark, and wait for the mark to land. This is what is termed as the memory mark, the one the dog has to remember if he is to successfully complete the double. Now turn your dog to the left to face the second mark.

Maybe now you see why having the belt cord attached is helpful. Most dogs will resist having their focus taken off the first mark, and you may need to use your belt cord to help reposition your dog into the proper heel position. Once he is properly set, signal for the second mark to be thrown. Wait a few seconds, and then send him on that retrieve. He is likely to go straight away and pick up that bumper. As he is returning to you, turn to face the first bumper thrown and have the dog get back into the heel position. Because you are on mowed ground and using a white bumper,

Cover will be a hindrance in initial multiple-mark training, as you want the dog to be able to see where the two bumpers land.

The dog awaits the command to retrieve one of the marks, which have been thrown to land at an angle of less than 90 degrees.

the dog should focus in on this mark right away. If he doesn't, give him a minute or two before having your assistant walk out and help him key in on the bumper. Once the dog is focused on the location, send him to make the retrieve.

Rerun this scenario at least two more times before moving on to something else. Reruns help improve the dog's use of memory through repetition. Another way to accomplish this is with what are sometimes termed rehearsals, in which the dog makes a number of retrieves (let's say six) of the same

mark. Then that mark is used as the memory bird of a subsequent double. Because the dog has run that exact mark prior to the double being thrown, he is more apt to focus on the successful completion of that retrieve and should meet with greater success.

If you find that your dog attempts to switch as he is heading for the first retrieve (his second mark), you need to prevent that switch from happening. The best way to do that is to have your assistant quickly run out and pick up the bumper before the dog can reach it. That will not be enough, though, as the dog needs to understand that switching is not allowed. You will have to chase your dog down and correct him for going to the wrong area, and you need to make the correction in that area where the bumper was thrown. That means if you don't catch him there, you need to forcefully take him there and then correct him. Once he is corrected, take him to the correct bumper and send him in to retrieve it. Now praise him and rerun the setup. If you made the proper correction, the dog is not likely to switch again.

Over time, you will both narrow and lengthen these double marks until the dog is making 100-yard double-marked retrieves at angles of less than 45 degrees on bare ground and seldom, if ever, attempting to switch. Once that milestone has been reached, you can move on to running doubles in cover.

The transition to cover should proceed along the same path taken for the single-marked retrieves. Work first in light cover and gradually move to heavier cover. Start with short, wide marks and lengthen them over time. When you begin to narrow your marks here, you are likely to have some problems with switching, so narrow the marks at a short distance before attempting longer, narrow double-marked retrieves. If your dog is having trouble with these early doubles in cover, you can spread a few bumpers out in the area of the two marks to make it easier for your dog to locate a bumper and be successful. However, I don't find that this needs to be done very often. By the time you are at this level of training, your dog is really starting to focus and needs less and less help. Still, if you feel it would improve your odds, you can employ this technique without any trepidation, but do not do so for long.

Once you move to cover, you may find that switching becomes more of a problem. The cover causes the dog to lose his mark

The dog runs to retrieve his first mark, which is actually the second bumper thrown.

The dog returns to his owner with his first retrieve; he will then be sent for the other mark.

more easily, and that can be a bit frustrating for some dogs. This frustration can lead to switching, as the dog gives up on locating the first mark he is sent to and switches to the opposite bird or bumper. Look at these situations as opportunities to correct the problem rather than simply as setbacks. You cannot teach your dog to not switch while in the field if he will not do so in training. So every time he switches is simply another opportunity to teach him not to.

For the average enthusiast, training a dog to make double-marked retrieves is likely enough. However, if you do a bit of duck hunting with your dog, you may want to train for triples or even quads. The process is the same as outlined for doubles; you are simply adding another layer of marks as you proceed through it.

Teaching the Conditioned Retrieve (Force Fetch)

Whether or not one should train his spaniel on a retrieve is another area of debate among the members of the hunting spaniel community. There are those who believe all retrieving should be natural, and only a natural retrieve should be encouraged, accepted, and developed in spaniels. Some of these natural retrieve supporters believe there is a risk of breeding out the natural retrieve of most spaniels once a majority of them are trained on a conditioned retrieve, commonly referred to as force broken. Then there are those who see the benefit to a conditioned retrieve and train nearly every spaniel they handle to the conditioned or trained retrieve. They believe that force breaking a dog to retrieve ensures a better retrieve and a more appropriate understanding in the dog's mind of his role within the team.

I fall into the latter category and dismiss the concerns of the former, but not without some apprehension. I believe that it is possible to breed out, intentionally or not, any trait, and for that reason I insist that a natural propensity for retrieving be shown to me prior to force breaking and, more important, prior to breeding. I would no more breed a field dog that did not like to retrieve than I would breed a dog that did not want to swim or could not find a bird in the field. There needs to be a good amount of the so-called natural retrieve in a dog both to make the force breaking go a bit easier and to make the dog a worthwhile subject for breeding, if that is intended to be a part of his lot in life. In short, I look upon the use of the conditioned retrieve as a means of enhancing a dog's field abilities and not as a way of correcting a dog's inabilities.

Force breaking is a systematic way of conditioning a dog to pick up, hold, and carry a bird on command. The command used most often is *fetch*, but it can really be any word you want as long as you are consistent in its usage. Where I see force breaking as a benefit is in training the dog that wants to drop birds as (or, worse yet, before) he gets to the handler, the dog that likes to switch when retrieving multiple marks, the dog that carries the bird all the way to the handler but refuses to give it up, and the dog that is a bit hard-mouthed. All of these problems may be averted or dealt with much more easily in the force-broken dog versus the natural retrieving spaniel.

Unfortunately, the techniques of the past and the language used regarding force breaking or developing the conditioned retrieve serve to turn a lot of people off. However, people need to look beyond the past and see what can be done today using gentler techniques and language. Force is still used today, but it is a milder and lesser amount of force than that often used in the past. "Force" should not be thought of as a bad word or action; after all, you apply force to open and close a car door. How much force you use

is simply up to you. Do you use just enough to get the job done (a gentle tug), or do you put extra oomph into it (a loud and harsh slam) to make a point? The amount of force used is up to you and your dog to determine.

GETTING STARTED ON THE CONDITIONED RETRIEVE

I don't usually begin to think about force breaking my dogs until they are about eight months old; I often hold off until they are closer to twice that. My preference is to have the dog well versed in the other aspects of the fieldwork first and to have a solid relationship of trust built up between the two of us before I begin to push him in a new direction. That means I want a dog that is solidly obedient, is retrieving well, and has shown that he is interested in birds and hunting. Once I have all of that and I want to move the dog to a higher plane, I begin to force break. If I am having some of the problems mentioned earlier (not holding bumpers well, a bit reluctant to give them up, and so on), then I may choose to do this work sooner, provided I have seen a lot of general interest in retrieving.

The only equipment needed for the conditioned retrieve is what is referred to as a retrieving buck. This is normally made of wood and can be purchased at most gundog supply houses. If you cannot find one there, you can purchase a wooden or plastic obedience training dumbbell at your local pet supply center. The retrieving buck is best for early force breaking and, at this stage, is preferred over those items typically retrieved in the field, such as birds or bumpers.

I train the bulk of the conditioned retrieve with my dogs on the ground, right where they will be most of their lives. Some force-breaking programs suggest or sometimes insist that this be done on a specially designed table. I have never found this to be necessary and would not suggest that the average owner put the time and money into building a table if he is only going to be training one dog every few years. However, having a table or other elevated platform available for the early conditioning is going to be a back saver and make the dog a bit more receptive to the work when you begin.

Once you start to work on the conditioned retrieve, you need to stick with it on a regular and daily basis. This is not a training program that can be turned on and off at whim. Two or three short daily sessions are best. Although in the beginning you can continue all of your regular training programs (obedience, quartering, and so forth)

as you progress with the conditioned retrieve, you will reach a point at which you should stop all other retrieving. Don't worry, it will only last for a short time. Up until now, your training has consisted of a lot of praise, but you are now entering a phase in which you have to up the level of praise. A simple "good boy" given intermittently is not going to cut it. Your dog must know that he is doing it right and that you are pleased with what he is doing. He has to be constantly encouraged and assured in order to progress comfortably.

The conditioned retrieve involves a set series of steps, each of which must be taken in sequence to reach the end result. Do not try to skip a step with the hope of forging ahead faster, or you will likely end up with a confused and untrained dog. The steps required are
- Take and hold
- Carry
- Reach
- Pick it up
- Transitioning

We will cover each of these steps, and this will culminate in a dog conditioned to retrieve on command.

TAKE AND HOLD

This is the one step for which I believe that having a table or platform on which you can stand the dog while you are first training can be a benefit. It certainly helps your back, as you do not have to stay bent over while you constantly work at getting your dog to accept the retrieving buck in his mouth and hold on to it. As many dogs are a bit apprehensive of being taken off the floor and put onto a small table or platform, the use of one helps keep some dogs more focused and less willing to battle with you.

For our purposes, I will assume that you are working with the dog on a small table. However, you can do all of these steps with the dog on the ground and sitting in the heel position. Put your dog on the table and stand at his right side. Take your gloved left hand and run your first three fingers under the dog's collar as you take a firm grip of it with your hand on the underside of the dog's neck. Place your thumb and pinkie finger on opposite sides of the dog's lower jaw. You will now be able to control the dog's head movement a bit and, by using the thumb and pinkie finger, to roll the skin surrounding the lower jaw over the bottom teeth as you apply a bit of pressure to get the dog to open his mouth. As you do this, tell the dog to "fetch," meaning, at this point, to open his mouth. Do just this one exercise for up to a half

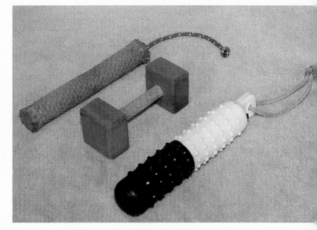

In the middle is a wooden retrieving buck, and to the left is a dowel that can also be used to teach the conditioned retrieve. The bumper (RIGHT) may be used as the training progresses.

dozen repetitions. Praise the dog well each time he opens his mouth, and release the grip within just a few seconds. You are simply trying to make the dog comfortable with having his mouth opened. If he struggles or fights you, simply keep working at it. Your grip on his collar gives you the power to keep him under control.

Once he seems comfortable with your opening his mouth, place your gloved right hand into his mouth so that he is able to grasp your hand across your palm, and tell him "hold." Continue to grip the collar with your left hand and continue to tell him to hold as you keep your right hand in his mouth. Do not

A tap under the chin serves as a correction if the dog tries to release the bumper before your command.

battle with him too much right now, just let him understand that he has to accept having your hand in his mouth.

After a few seconds, tell him "give" and remove your right hand as you offer a great deal of praise. Repeat these steps for about six repetitions. That is it; your first session is done! You will repeat this process during the next training session. As you progress, you should see the dog begin to fight the insertion of your gloved hand less and less; if he does not relent, take a gentle hold of his lower jaw with your right hand, and repeat the *hold*

command as you help him understand that he cannot spit out your hand—or, eventually, anything else. Once the dog is easily accepting your opening his mouth and will take your right hand in his mouth with little concern, it is time to introduce the retrieving buck.

Before beginning to work with the retrieving buck, let the dog sniff it and become acquainted with it, but do not use it as a retrieving tool or a toy. This is going to be a special tool used only for the conditioned retrieve. Now take hold of the dog's collar and open his mouth as described earlier. With the retrieving buck in your right hand, bring the buck to the dog's mouth in a way that lets him see the buck coming at him and allows you to easily insert the buck into his mouth so that an end of the buck is on each side of his mouth. As the buck is inserted into his mouth, tell the dog "hold." Undoubtedly, he will want to spit the buck out of his mouth, so keep your right hand near to be able to correct him. Correcting for attempting to spit the buck out is done by repeating the command *hold* and then giving a firm tap under the lower jaw every time he attempts to drop the buck. If the dog should succeed in spitting out the buck, you should simply say "no!" and reinsert the buck with a firm "fetch!" and "hold!" followed by praise. Be firm in your corrections here, but not overly zealous. Simply make your point known, and praise when he does it right.

As a means of avoidance, the dog will probably try to do a number of things, including lying down, jumping off the table, and turning his head as you reach for the collar, as well as myriad other things; when these types of avoidance happen, simply work through them. If he lies down, have him sit back up. If he jumps off the table (which he should not be able to do because you should have a

hold of his collar), put him back on it. If he should try to look away as you go to insert the buck, use your left hand to turn his head back around.

Remember that you need to ease the dog into holding the buck for longer and longer periods of time. Once he will hold it without the need for a correction, start stepping away from the table as you tell him to hold. Introduce small distractions, and try to get him to not drop the buck without being told "give." If he does drop it, step in and correct as described earlier. If you have never done this sort of training before, you will be surprised at how quickly you

Refresher Course

As you move ahead to each step in the force-fetch process, remember to come back to the previous step on a fairly frequent basis. That means that when you are working on the *carry*, revisit the *take* and *hold*, or when you are working on the *reach*, revisit the *carry*. This helps you maintain the basis from which you are progressing and gives the dog the confidence that he can do things right.

can get through this step, but you must make certain that he understands he is to hold the buck for as long as you want him to without fail before you can move forward.

CARRY

Although it may seem like simple transference from holding the buck while the dog is sitting still to holding it while he is moving—especially since this is what he has done every time he has retrieved for you—it does not turn out to be that simple a process. To start this,

you will need the dog on his training leash and collar. Have him sit in the heel position and put him through a small series of *fetch* and *give* commands before moving ahead. By the way, at this point you should use the *hold* command only as reinforcement or when needing to correct the dog.

Now tell the dog "heel" and begin having him move along with you. If he drops the buck—or maybe I should say *when* he drops the buck—stop and reinsert it with his *fetch* command. Look at his failure to hold properly while heeling as a training opportunity and not as a problem. He cannot learn to carry properly without making mistakes and learning what is wrong. As he moves along without dropping the buck, praise him and continue to reinforce the hold by repeating that command. Move only in short spurts at first, and increase the hold time gradually as you move along. Vary when you will take the buck from him so that he does not come to expect you to take it every time or every other time that you stop.

You also need to practice *come*s with him properly carrying the buck. Do this as you would any other *come*, simply make sure that he has the buck in his mouth the entire time. If he drops it—and he

The dog has to learn to move with the bumper in his mouth, carrying it the entire time.

will—move in and correct; praise well when he does it correctly. Throughout your training session, have him sometimes carry and sometimes not. Have him do a series of *fetch* and *give* commands, and generally mix things up as you would do during any obedience session, always remembering to lavish him with praise when he is doing what is expected of him.

At this point, you have gotten to where many people will either give up or simply say "good enough." However, if you truly want a finished gundog, you need to forge ahead; let's give it a go.

REACH

When your dog has completed the previous two steps and has learned the meaning of *fetch*, *hold*, and *give*, plus he reliably carries a buck without dropping it, you have done the sequence of *fetch* and *give* so many times that he is probably beginning to open his mouth as you reach for his collar or as he sees the buck coming at him. If that is the case, rejoice! You are well on your way, and he is getting conditioned to his role in the process.

Your goal now is to have him open his mouth on the word *fetch* without your assistance and, eventually, to reach out and grab the buck as it comes at him or is set in front of him. You will use force to teach him to open his mouth on the word *fetch*. Remember, though, that you will use just enough force to gain compliance and not so much to cause excessive discomfort; you are opening a door here, not slamming one shut. Although there are a number of ways in which to apply force, I recommend only two methods, as I find the others to be unacceptable or otherwise lacking in some way.

The two methods recommended are the ear pinch and the lip fold, with the latter being my preferred method. When applying the ear pinch, you grasp the tiny fold of the ear near the ear's base and pinch it between your thumb and forefinger, driving your thumbnail into the skin with just enough force to get the dog to open his mouth. The lip fold is simply an extension of what was done to open the mouth earlier, only now you apply a sufficient amount of force against the teeth to cause the dog to quickly open his mouth. The lip fold allows you to control the head, gives a good and recognizable look at the buck when you tell the dog to fetch, and permits you to adjust the level of force more easily. Once you have decided on the type of force you will use in the process, it is time to move along.

Begin with your dog sitting in the heel position. With the buck in your right hand, bring it toward the dog, and as it gets directly in front of the dog's muzzle, say "fetch." If he opens his mouth and takes the buck, praise him. If he fails to open his mouth, reach down with your left hand and apply force as you say "fetch," insert the buck, and praise. Once the dog consistently opens his mouth every time you give the *fetch* command, it is time to have him start reaching for the buck.

I like to start the dog reaching as he is heeling along beside me. The action of moving forward toward the buck is mimicked by the motion of heeling, and there appears to be a higher level of success from this process. To do this, have the dog heel beside you without carrying the buck. Then, using your right hand, bring the buck in front of the dog's muzzle as you are moving along and tell him "fetch." He will likely simply open his mouth and grab the buck, at which time you praise—a lot. If he fails to grab the buck, quickly reach down with your left hand, apply force, and insert the buck as you continue to move. He will quickly pick up on this exercise and gladly reach for the buck while heeling. Now it is time to have the dog reach for the buck from a stationary position.

The ear pinch provides an appropriate amount of discomfort in teaching the dog to take the bumper.

The eventual goal is for the dog to reach out and take the bumper without your assistance.

With the dog sitting in the heel position, bring the buck in front of his muzzle with your right hand, only this time stop a couple of inches in front of the muzzle as you give the *fetch* command. If he reaches and takes the buck, be sure to praise him. If he fails, then use your left hand to push his head forward, toward the buck, as you say "no—fetch"; any further resistance should be met with an application of force. After a few such sessions, your dog will likely understand that he has to fetch even if he has to reach for the buck. Continue with this process until he seldom refuses, and then begin to slowly lengthen the distance and vary the angle (up, down, to the right, to the left, and so on) where he must reach to get the buck.

Just as you encountered a few attempts at avoidance with the initial part of this process, you may encounter some here as well. Head turning is a common problem, but the way to deal with it is a bit different from what was done before. At this point, the dog is beyond your merely gently repositioning his head. He is now to the point where he needs a correction with the application of your force method and a firm "no—fetch."

Another form of avoidance is when the dog begins to grab the buck before being told. Just as in steadiness drills, where you correct for anticipation of a command, you need to correct the dog if he reaches for the buck before being told to fetch. What he is really doing here is attempting to avoid the application of force, but you need to let him understand that force is not applied unless there is failure to retrieve, and retrieving is not to be done until told. So if this happens, give him a firm "no," and prevent him from taking the buck prematurely.

PICK IT UP

You are now at the threshold with your dog. He is about to realize that you have the power to control his retrieve and that he must comply. Once that is solidly ingrained in his psyche, he will begin to give you crisper retrieves. The little annoyances of dropped birds, refusals, and poor delivery will begin to be things of the past. However, you still have one more hurdle to clear.

You have just finished conditioning the dog to reach for the buck but not yet to reach out and pick the buck up off the ground. To do that, begin with the dog in the heel position, and have him reach for and fetch the buck from a distance of about 2 feet directly in front of his muzzle. Next, hold the buck closer to the ground but not yet on the ground as you give the *fetch* command. Remember to praise when he does it right and correct when he does it wrong, using the same methods outlined in the last step of this process. Continue to follow this slow progression to the ground until you are holding the buck on the ground as you give the *fetch* command. Do not remove your hand from the buck until the dog grabs it. Continue to follow this process for several repetitions, remembering to always praise well when it is deserved and correct appropriately when needed.

Once the dog is willing to consistently snatch the buck from the ground, albeit with you still holding onto it, you can go back to having him fetch the buck as you are heeling him, just as you did when you started to have him reach for the buck in the previous step. Now, however, you will start to hold the buck about halfway to the ground when you hold it in front of the dog, rather than directly in front of his muzzle. After he is successfully grabbing the buck in that position, you can occasionally drop the buck on the ground a few feet ahead of him as he heels, giving the *fetch* command as you do. In all likelihood, he will snatch the buck from the ground and keep moving.

However, if he fails, you will have to step in and correct him with force and take him to the buck for a pickup.

At this point, your dog should be conditioned well enough to consistently fetch the buck from the ground while heeling. Now return to the stationary position with your dog in the heel position. Toss the buck in front of the dog where he can plainly see it, and give him the *fetch* command. If he does not pick it up, correct as you have been. Praise him when he has it in his mouth and move on. Repeat the sequence over and over until he is consistently fetching the buck, whether moving at heel or sitting at your side. The dog has now progressed to the point at which he needs to fetch from a variety of angles and distances. This is a good time to begin to move the buck out a few more feet every time and to begin to add different angles by tossing the buck to either side of the dog rather than directly in front of him.

TRANSITIONING

You now have the task of transitioning from the retrieving buck to bumpers and birds. All that the transitioning process entails is a substitution of the buck with either a bumper or a bird, and you may be surprised at how your dog will balk at fetching those items without some transition work done to help things along. The transition process begins at the *reach* stage and progresses through *pick it up*. You should find that the transition will go smoothly and quickly, as your dog is probably in a more cooperative state after all that you have done with him. As always, to be successful you need to be consistent with your methods and stick to the program. From now on, any time your dog refuses or hesitates to retrieve, tell him "fetch," apply your normal force if necessary, and say "give" to have him release the bird.

The end result of force-fetch is a dog that should never refuse a retrieve and should always deliver the bird to hand.

The finished dog is alert and responsive in the field,
in tune to you and your commands.

The Finished Dog: Advanced Training

At this point in your training, you are at the polishing-up stage. This is when you will fine-tune many of the elements that your dog has already learned. His retrieves will be crisper, his flushes will likely be bolder, and his response to your commands will be more consistent, but you are not yet done with training. There are still a few things that the hunting spaniel needs to learn to truly become a finished gundog, and the first of those is how to handle a blind retrieve.

The definition of a blind retrieve is the retrieve of a bird that the dog does not see fall and, therefore, has not been able to mark. The dog's ability to recover the bird is dependent upon his training and willingness to be handled (directed or steered to the bird through voice, arm, and whistle signals given by the handler) to the area of the fall. In spanieldom, there exist two forms of blind retrieves.

Unique to spaniels is the concept of what is called the hunt dead retrieve. The hunt dead is a retrieve that is accomplished by having the dog quarter through an area at a distance that usually exceeds typical gun range in the hopes of coming

This dog has been sent to complete a hunt dead. He will quarter, perhaps out of gun range, until he comes across the dead bird and makes the retrieve.

across the downed bird. Personally, I am opposed to the use of the hunt dead and find it practical only when the handler has been unable to identify the location of the bird's fall and knows that the bird is down within relatively close proximity, in other words, within gun range. If either of these two conditions does not exist, I believe it is best to retrieve the bird by having the dog complete a common blind retrieve or by simply quartering through the area of the fall with the dog. The

hunt dead has the potential of disturbing a lot of ground unnecessarily and scaring other birds out of the area or having them flush while you are lounging out of gun range. None of these will put more game in your bag. Still, the hunt dead has a modicum of usefulness and for that reason will be discussed later.

Then there is the common blind retrieve; this is the retrieve of a bird that you marked but your dog did not. Through training, you teach your dog to follow your directions by responding to hand and arm signals that direct him along a specific line until he has come to the bird. In running a blind retrieve, the dog must be able to stop on command and be cast to one side or the other as well as farther back. This retrieve is useful when a bird has dropped a considerable distance from the handler or is across some kind of barrier, such as a creek or a fence line.

Every spaniel should be trained to do rudimentary blind retrieves. Spaniels that may be used extensively as nonslip retrievers will be better off to receive advanced blind retrieve training involving a variety of drills that are beyond the scope of this book. Look to retriever training books for more information concerning such training drills.

In addition to blind retrieves, we'll discuss honoring and hunting in braces in this chapter to round out your spaniel's training.

Teaching the Hunt Dead

Training the dog to hunt dead is a rather easy task that can actually begin shortly after you have completed your quartering work and marked retrieves. Begin working on bare ground. While heeling the dog through the area, nonchalantly drop a bumper or dead bird behind you while the dog is focused on other things. Continue to heel him about another 10 yards or so, and then turn around and face the bumper. Once you see him focused on the bumper, tell him "hunt dead" and let him go. He will probably run out and pick up the bumper or bird without hesitation. Praise him and move on. Now, begin to incorporate this little exercise into your daily training routine.

As time progresses, increase the distance that you heel the dog after you have dropped the bumper until you are out to about 30 yards. At that point, you can begin to run this exercise in light cover, starting with short distances and gradually increasing them to around 30 yards. Follow this progression through the various types of cover, and increase the distance to as much as 60 yards. For a dog to successfully complete the hunt dead, he has to be able to find the bird; in anything more than light cover, he will need to use his nose to do that. Therefore, I like to use only birds for hunt dead drills once I have the dog working in medium and heavy cover. Always remember to send your dog straight away from you and not at any sort of angle. Because of the quartering work that you have taught the dog, you should find that your dog will begin to quarter when he gets about 20 or so yards away from you in cover. This is a good thing, and it shows that the dog is seeking game rather than simply running out in the field.

Teaching the Common Blind Retrieve

There is a reason that you have waited until now to teach the flushing dog blind retrieves. The flushing dog's primary objective is to locate and flush birds in the field. This requires the dog to efficiently quarter a field and respond to commands. To efficiently complete a blind retrieve, however, the dog has to run as direct a route as possible to get to the area of the fall. Part of your job as trainer is to help the dog learn to run a fairly straight line to a blind. This puts the two objectives at odds with one another. Because the primary objective is to have the dog quartering a field, that is the one we concentrate on and ingrain first. If we were to train the blind before solidifying the dog's quartering ability, we would expect mediocre fieldwork. That might be fine and acceptable for, say, a nonslip retriever trying to work as a flushing dog, but it is unacceptable for a spaniel whose primary purpose is going to be to flush birds before the gun.

The *back* arm signal.

There is a common set of verbal and arm signals used with blind retrieves, so let's address those right now. It is useful to help your dog distinguish between being sent on a blind retrieve and being sent for a marked retrieve. With that in mind, the following verbal commands are given to a dog when he is sent to retrieve a blind:

Dead—with your dog in the heel position, give this command to tell the dog that this will be a blind retrieve.

Line—when your dog focuses in the direction you want to send him, give this command to tell him that he has the right idea.

Back—this is the command used to send your dog to the blind. (Note: do not send the dog on his name; that is done only on a marked retrieve.)

As mentioned earlier, the successful completion of a blind retrieve requires that the dog take a relatively straight line to the area of the fall. Since it is often the case that the dog does not peg the blind (go straight to it and practically step on the bird), the dog also needs to be able to stop on command and respond to directions to go left or right, go farther back, or come in closer to you. To do this, you will use a series of the following verbal, whistle, and arm signals to direct your dog.

Back—this tells the dog to go farther back from the spot he is sitting on. You want the dog to turn around and start moving deeper into the field. The arm signal is given by thrusting an arm straight up from your shoulder with the palm flat and fingers extended. If you have just completed giving the dog an *over*, say to the right, you will use the opposite arm, in this case your left, to send him farther back.

Come-in (whistle: *tweet-tweet-tweet-tweet-tweet*)—this tells the dog that he has gone too far and needs to come back in closer to you. The arm signal is a combination of you bending over slightly and dropping one arm down as you shake your hand a little to attract the dog toward you.

Over—this tells the dog to go left or right based upon the arm signal given in conjunction with this verbal command. The arm signal is given by thrusting your arm out at shoulder level in whichever direction you are intending to send the dog. For example, to send the dog to the right, you would say "over" and fully extend your right arm at shoulder level in that direction.

Sit (whistle: *tweeeet*)—tells the dog to sit and turn to look at you. (Note: Do not use "hup" here, as you could create confusion in the field.

The *come-in* arm signal.

The *over* arm signal.

The *hup* command does not require the dog to turn and face you.)

As you can see, you will be teaching the dog how to complete a number of individualized tasks: come-in, over, back, sit, and so forth. By combining these tasks into one series of sequences, you can execute a blind retrieve. However, it will not be as easy as it might sound because, as we all know, once we get to the field all manner of distractions and obstacles come into play. For that reason, you will always have to drill your dog not only on the rudimentary commands shown here but also on a variety of drills meant to build and maintain confidence in the dog.

THE BASICS OF THE BLIND RETRIEVE

The first element of training the blind retrieve involves getting your dog to take a line to the blind. To do this, you will want to have a visual aid that is easy for the dog to see, whether the marker is close up or far away. There are a variety of markers used for this, including a white bucket, white traffic cone, and white or white-and-black flags. I like to use flags as my markers, as they are easier to handle in the field and can also be used in water when you progress to practicing in water.

As always, you will begin on bare ground, and you should choose an unobstructed location for the blind. Place your marker where you want the blind to be, then grab about six bumpers and heel your dog to within a few yards of the marker. With the dog sitting in the heel position, toss a bumper in front of the marker as you say "dead"; do this for every bumper until they are all placed in front of the marker. Now turn and heel your dog about 20 yards away, then turn him to face the marker and the pile of bumpers.

With the dog in the heel position, tell him "dead" to begin having him understand that this is a new type of retrieve. As he focuses on the marker, tell him "line." This says, "Yes, you are looking where I want you to look." It will take some time for him to understand this completely. Quickly give him the command *back*. He may hesitate to go when he hears *back*; if that is the case, simply encourage him. Once he knows he can make the retrieve upon hearing this new command, he will move out quickly. Repeat this sequence one more time for a second retrieve. As the dog is going out for the second bumper, turn and move back another 20 or so yards, then turn and face the marker. Your dog will be heading back to you with the bumper. When he gets back in the heel position, praise him and send him on another retrieve. Again, repeat this sequence, and then move back another 20 yards. You are now out about 60 yards from the marker, and your dog has retrieved four of the six bumpers. Have him make the next two retrieves, and end the session.

Retrieves set up like this are referred to as pattern blinds, and you want to repeat these pattern blinds several times and in many different locations—still on bare ground—until your dog is consistently retrieving bumpers from in front of a marker at a distance of 100 yards. After the first few days of running this sequence, you can increase the number of bumpers used to about a dozen. Although you do not need to do any more than two training sessions per day, adding a third whenever you have the opportunity will simply speed this process along.

No

It is now time to teach the dog that you are the one who will select the pile he is to retrieve from. You need to do this because there will be times when your dog will not focus his attention in the right direction. When that happens, you want to be able to tell him "no" and draw his

Here are three ways to mark your bumper pile. On the left, a flag is hooked into an electric fence post (available at most farm-supply stores) and works well in tall cover. The other flag and bucket work well on bare ground and in low cover.

attention to the correct area. At this point, you will introduce a second marker and, thereby, a second retrieving pile. Choose the location from which you will send the dog. Place one marker 100 yards out, then place a second marker 100 yards out but at a 90-degree angle to the first marker. By this time, your dog should know to quickly focus in on the marker, and you can dispense with the shorter early marks. Therefore, you will be making 100-yard retrieves right from the start.

Line the dog up facing one of the markers and send him for a retrieve. Have him bring the bumper

Depiction of how bumpers can be set around a visual aid to begin the process of teaching the dog to run a blind.

back, and make sure he returns to the heel position before you have him give you the bumper. After taking the bumper, heel the dog around for a moment, and then return to your chosen location. Have the dog face the last marker you sent him to and say "no" firmly but not harshly. Now tell the dog to heel, and pivot to face the second marker.

Send him to the second marker. Because of the wide angle between the two markers and because you have worked on switch problems already, it is likely that the dog will go straight out and pick up the bumper. When he returns, make sure he gets to the heel position before you have him give you the bumper. After taking the

bumper, have the dog face the last marker you sent him to and say "no." Now tell the dog to heel, and pivot to face the other marker. Send your dog, and continue to follow this back-and-forth sequence until all of the bumpers have been picked up.

If he happens to head for the wrong bumper, your correction will be like that used for switching, discussed in an earlier chapter. I do not usually see a dog trying to go to the wrong marker until I place the cones at less of an angle from one another. You can start doing that after you have had several sessions in various locations (have you noticed a theme here?) with the cones placed 90 degrees apart.

Move your markers closer together in small increments to increase the chances of success and decrease the likelihood of failure. Of course, your dog will have to commit a few transgressions to understand exactly what he is supposed to do, but keeping them at a minimum will help build his confidence. Do not get carried away with the angle of separation. The markers need not be any closer than about 25 to 35 degrees.

At this time, your dog will have a fairly good idea that in this setting, "no" means to ignore a specific pile, marker, or bird.

Once the dog is successfully completing pattern blinds using two markers set no closer than about 25 degrees apart, you can introduce a third marker/pile to the mix. To begin, set the markers/piles with about 45 degrees between each other; as the dog progresses, you can move the markers closer or farther apart, but never with more than about 90 degrees or less than about 25 degrees separating them. As with all training, mix things up a bit by constantly selecting a different retrieving sequence to keep the dog focused on your commands.

Depiction of how a flag attached to a plastic electric fence post can aid a dog in locating the pile of bumpers when transitioning to heavy cover.

WEANING

You are now at a point at which you can begin to wean the dog from the need for the markers, at least on bare ground. To start this process, set up a single marker about 100 yards out from your starting point, and place six white or white-and-black bumpers in front of it. Have the dog retrieve the first five bumpers. Now, before sending him to get the sixth one, walk out and remove the marker. Be sure to put it where the dog cannot see it. Return to the dog, and send him to pick up the last bumper. He will likely go directly to the pile area and find the sixth bumper. During the next few training sessions, you will repeat this process a few times and then have the dog retrieve just the first four bumpers before you remove the marker. Take a couple of sessions to get the dog used to this sequence, and then repeat the process a few more times and have the dog retrieve just the first three bumpers. Once you can consistently send the dog to retrieve the last three bumpers without the marker in place, begin using solid black bumpers instead of the white or white-and-black ones. The dog will have a harder time seeing the solid black bumpers and will have to rely on memory and the confidence he has in you to successfully complete the retrieve.

Once the dog has progressed to retrieving solid black bumpers in simple pattern blinds such as these, you can begin to use a few black bumpers mixed in with your white or white-and-black bumpers when working with multiple markers. At this point, you can also begin to remove an occasional marker from a two- or three-marker mix just as you did for the single marker pattern blind.

Now you are ready to push your dog to a fuller understanding of *no* and to have greater confidence in your decisions. Place two markers at about a 45-degree angle to one another, and establish

The dog is sent to a pile of bumpers and makes a retrieve.

a pile of three black bumpers at each marker. Have him pick up two bumpers from each pile, and then go and remove one of the two markers. Have him face the one remaining marker and tell him "no." Turn him in the direction of the other pile and command "dead—line—back." He should go to the pile that is missing its marker, but he will be very tempted to go to the pile with the visible marker instead. If he does that, correct him as you did for switching. Persevere and be consistent with this drill. You need to teach him to go where you tell him and not to where he sees a patch of white. That is what he is learning here: to listen to you and not his eyes.

MOVING TO COVER

Moving to cover here is little different from how it was done with marked retrieves. Because the dog is already accustomed to marked retrieves in cover and to the concept of white markers that help him locate the pile, you can simply move right into any type of cover you choose. The only caution here is that you need to make certain that the marker is visible to the dog. If the cover is so thick that the marker cannot be seen, then raise the marker higher so that the dog can see it, and place the bumpers at its base. When you are running these drills in cover, if your dog seems to be having trouble, get down at his eye level and check out the visibility. You might find that the problem does not lie with the dog but lies with the setup. If that is the case, adjust the setup as needed.

WATER

Everything you do on land can be done in water with only a few caveats. First, do not establish early pattern blinds that require the dog to go through water and then onto shore to get to the pile. Save this work for later in the game, when you are certain your dog will not run the bank. Second, keep your angles wide when working with multiple markers. Third, have your dog's entry be square to the water's edge rather than angled, if at all possible. All the steps you followed for lining your dog to a pile can be done in the water.

I mentioned earlier that I like to use flags as markers. When you come to this water work, you'll find flags easy and practical to use. A flag mounted on a long pole can be easily placed in water that is 3 to 4 feet deep, whereas a traffic cone or a bucket cannot.

Your spaniel should respond eagerly when you move your training into the water.

CASTING

To maintain a consistent training methodology and build confidence in your dog, you will want to use markers to teach casting. I do not recommend starting these drills until the dog has become familiar with running to a pile to make a retrieve, so you should wait until your dog has done about a week or so of lining drills and is confidently retrieving from a pile. Once that is happening, you can train your dog to line to a pile and take casts in parallel.

As with other retrieve training, you want to begin on bare ground. There will be four casts taught during this process, and they will be taught one at a time. Let's begin with the *back* cast. This is the cast that tells the dog to turn away

The use of a visual aid helps draw the dog across a body of water and into heavy cover on the other side in preparation for running a blind retrieve across water.

from you and head farther out in the field.

Picture the dog sitting some 50 yards out from you, unable to locate a bird. You know the bird is another 30 yards out from the dog and directly in line with you. What do you do? When the dog comes directly in line with you and the bird, blow your *stop* whistle and

have him sit facing you. Pause and give the dog the opportunity to focus in on you. Now raise your right arm straight up from the shoulder with your palm flat and fingers pointed upward as you say "back." The dog, knowing this signal, turns around and heads straight away, waiting to hear another signal or come upon a bird. Soon he picks up scent and finds the downed bird. He quickly snatches the bird from the ground and rushes back to your side with the retrieve. You and the dog have just executed a perfect *back* cast.

To teach the *back* cast, locate a spot in an open mowed field from which you will be sending your dog. Walk about 30 yards out into the field and place a marker. Get your dog and heel him to a location that is 20 yards from where you will be standing and between you and the marker. With the dog sitting at heel and facing the marker, toss six white or white-and-black bumpers, one at a time, so that they land just in front of the marker. Tell your dog to heel, and pivot around to face the opposite direction, looking directly at the spot from which you will be casting your dog. Have your dog stay, and return to your location.

Turn to face your dog and, after a moment's pause, raise your right arm straight up from the shoulder with your palm flat and fingers pointed upward as you say "back." Because of the preliminary work you have done while teaching the dog to take a line, he knows that the word *back* means to go to the marker and retrieve a bumper. True enough, the marker is now at his back rather than in front of him, but this is of little concern. The dog turns, runs to the pile, and retrieves a bumper. You praise wildly and then walk him back to his spot to rerun the exercise. Repeat the exercise until all bumpers are picked up. Work only the *back* command for about three or four days, then add a *side* cast.

Let's take a moment to go back to our earlier *back* cast scenario and consider this time that the bird, instead of being farther down the field, is actually off to the right side of the dog, and the dog is simply not getting far enough to the right to find the bird. What do you do? You stop the dog and then give him a *right over* cast that drives him to the bird.

To teach a *side* cast, use the same setup as you did for the *back* cast, except now place the flag 10 yards to either the immediate left or right of the dog. For our purposes here, we will assume that you will place the flag to the right. Again, take the dog to his spot and

have him face the flag. Toss six bumpers in front of it, and then tell the dog to heel as you pivot to face the area from which you will cast the dog. Return to your spot, turn to face your dog, and pause for a moment, then extend your arm directly to the right, palm open flat and fingers pointed, as you say "over." The dog will turn toward the flag and make a retrieve. Heel the dog back to his location, and then repeat the exercise until all the bumpers have been picked up.

At this point, you can train both the *back* cast and the *right over* cast in parallel but separate from one another. After about three or four days of repetition, begin to teach the *left over* cast using the same setup as with the *right over*, only to the opposite side. Once the dog has completed a few *left over* casts successfully, you can train the *back*, *right over*, and *left over* casts in parallel but still separate from one another.

Finally, it is time to train the *come-in* cast. In this cast, the pile is not marked and is located directly between you and the dog. It is taught so that should your dog overshoot a retrieve and end up farther out than he should be, you can have him come in to you and know to look for a bird along the way. Set your dog up on his spot, facing where you will be located, then toss six bumpers into a pile about halfway between the dog and where you will be located as you direct him. Blow the *come-in* whistle, and don't forget to bend over slightly as you drop one arm down and shake your hand a little to attract the dog toward you. When he gets to the pile, he will pick up a bumper and retrieve it to you. As always, heel him back to his spot and repeat the exercise until all bumpers are picked up. As before, continue to work this new command for about three or four days of repetition and in tandem but still as separate

Further Training

As was stated earlier, this book is written primarily as a primer for the flushing gundog and not as an instruction manual for training a non-slip retriever. There are a number of other handling drills that can be utilized to make your dog more proficient and to improve your handling skills. If you wish to learn more, please explore the many publications available to those who want a non-slip retriever.

exercises with the *back*, *right over*, and *left over* casts.

Once the dog has had a rudimentary introduction to the casts, you can expand the training process. Instead of setting up just one marker, set up three, positioning one about 10 yards to the left, another 10 yards to the right, and the third about 10 yards behind where the dog will be set (sitting). However, just because you have three markers out, do not establish three piles. Your piles will be established only as you need them for each particular cast. For instance, let's say you are going to train the *left over* first. You go out and establish the *left over* pile. Now run your dog on that cast until all bumpers have been picked up. Next, establish the pile for the next cast, let's say the *back*, and run your dog on that cast until all the bumpers have been picked up. Continue this process until you have worked through all of the casts. For the next several training sessions, continue to put up three markers but establish only one pile at a time. The reason for doing this is that if the dog decides to go to the wrong marker, he is not going to find a bumper. This makes him more reliant upon your direction rather than on his thinking that he can take matters into his own hands. After you have run enough sessions to be confident that the dog will perform the correct cast when told, move on to the next drill.

Because some dogs try to anticipate a rerun of the last cast given, begin to place one bumper in front of each marker and for the *come-in* cast. This keeps the dog from finding a bumper at the last cast completed if he decides to anticipate a rerun. Have the dog complete one of each of the types of casts and then reset the setup and repeat, but do not give the casts in the same order. After several sessions like this, you can begin to establish piles of just three bumpers per station and to lengthen the casts out to as much as about 30 yards for the *over*s and 50 yards for the *back*. In addition, begin to mix in black bumpers with the white or white-and-black ones. Over the course of the next few days, you can eliminate the white ones altogether and use just black bumpers.

When the dog is reliably completing each cast, you can begin to wean him from the markers altogether. I like to wean the side markers first and the back marker last because that is the farthest from the dog. Once the dog is weaned off the markers, you can move to casting drills in cover. The same rules will apply there that apply with the lining drills. Start out in cover using

The *stop* whistle tells the dog to turn and face you rather than sit by your side.

markers, but be sure that they are visible to the dog. Stop using markers as soon as you can, but do not be afraid to resort to them if need be. Be certain to vary the training locations, terrain, cover type, and wind direction as often as you can to ensure that your dog gets every opportunity to learn these tasks in all types of environments.

TEACHING THE DOG TO STOP

By the time you have reached the point at which you can begin to teach the blind retrieve, your dog should already be stopping on a whistle. The only difference between this stop and a spaniel hup is that you want the dog to turn and face you rather than sit and watch for a bird to drop. Remember that the dog will have been sent on a blind retrieve, and he will know that because you will have sent him by saying "dead—line—back." So the dog has the ability to differentiate between a stop while quartering and a stop while working a blind retrieve.

When first using the *stop* whistle during a blind retrieve sequence, blow the whistle and give the *sit* command; if the dog did not turn to face you, give him a *come* whistle. As he turns to come, give him another *stop* whistle and praise when he stops. He will soon begin to anticipate that when you have him stop during a blind retrieve, he is to turn and face you. This is also why I carry two different whistles with me while hunting. Using a retriever rather than a spaniel whistle for blind retrieves can also help the dog differentiate between the two *stop* whistles.

TRANSITIONING TO TRUE BLIND RETRIEVES

Your dog has learned to
- take a line out to about 100 yards;
- be told to ignore one possible retrieve and accept another;
- respond to a set of verbal, whistle, and arm signals; and
- allow himself to be directed to a specific area simply because you want him there.

Now your dog is ready to transition to truly blind retrieves. I like to begin this transition process by developing a series of permanent blinds. These are blind retrieves of various lengths that are run over and over again in the same location and from the same spot. They are begun as all of the pattern blinds were with the use of a marker to guide the dog to the spot. However, the markers are quickly eliminated; now the only thing the dog will have to guide him is his memory.

These pattern blinds help to establish and maintain the dog's confidence in himself and in you. If he feels confident that every time he takes the line to a specific perma-nent blind he is going to find a bumper, he is more likely to be willing to take a line every time one is given. When he understands that you send him only when there truly is something there to retrieve, he is more likely to accept your guidance. I suggest that you establish and maintain a total of six permanent blinds that vary in length from 50 to 125 yards and vary in type of terrain, cover, and common wind direction.

After the dog is successfully completing the permanent blind retrieves on a regular basis, begin to give him real blinds. To do this, locate an area of light to moderate cover and find a good spot in which to set three bumpers. After placing the bumpers, get your dog and heel him to a spot that is approximately 50 yards from the bumpers and where the wind is at your back. Line your dog up in the direction of the bumpers and tell him "dead." His eyes should focus straight ahead; if they don't, tell him "no" and get him focusing forward with "line" and "back." He should be heading in a relatively straight line toward the bumpers; if he veers off too far to the right or the left, give him a *stop* whistle. Wait a moment and let him concentrate. Now give him either a *left* or *right over* to bring him back in line with the location of the bumpers. Once he is there, give him another *stop* whistle. He should now be in front of the bumpers, so all you should need to do is give him a *back* command to drive him straight back to the bumpers. When he gets a bumper, have him retrieve it to the heel position, and praise the heck out of him.

Rerun the blind. He will probably do better this time because he

Your dog must display the proper etiquette and behavior when hunting with others.

has a better idea of where he is going. Handle him when and if necessary, and praise him when he brings that next bumper in. Now go do something else—maybe give him a few marks or practice his quartering skills. Wait about ten or fifteen minutes, and then return to the site to rerun that blind one last time. What you are doing here is testing his memory and his willingness to trust you.

Continue to run him on his permanent blinds and at least one new 50-yard blind nearly every day over the course of a week or more. As he gets more and more reliable on these short blinds, it is time to step up the distance and push him

Hunting in a brace, meaning that two dogs work together, requires each dog to honor the other's work.

lane, simply frame a lane by making a fist with one hand and extending the pinkie and index fingers. Now extend your arm and look through the frame of those fingers toward the blind with the blind centered between them. The outside boundaries of the lane are now seen and framed by your two fingers. If your dog gets far outside of this lane, you need to stop him and cast him either right or left to have him return to the center of the lane. Then cast him back toward the blind.

Continue to increase the length of the new blinds incrementally until you have reached a distance of 125 yards. Don't forget to maintain your work with the permanent blinds as well. Any longer distances that you care to work at are really of your choosing. By the time you have been able to have your dog consistently completing blind retrieves out to 125 yards, steady to wing and shot and making multiple marked retrieves, your dog can well be considered a finished gundog.

Honoring

I have not yet talked about honoring, but it is high time that I do. When a dog honors, he respects another dog's work by remaining in place and not stealing—also known as poaching—or attempting to steal the other dog's retrieve or chasing

deeper by increasing the new blind to 75 yards. As you lengthen the blind, you may find him balking at about 50 yards because you have been doing so many at that distance. Try to let him work through this on his own; if he absolutely gives up, have him stop on the whistle, and give him a *back* command to drive him deeper.

Always work at keeping him in the retrieving lane so that he does not end up wandering all over the field. To determine if he is in the

after the other dog's flush. If you and your dog will ever hunt with another person and his dog, you need to teach your dog to honor. To do so is simple, especially once you have gotten your dog steady to wing and shot or steady at the line.

Begin to practice honoring with thrown marks. All you need for such practice is another handler and dog along with someone to throw the marks. Set the two dogs up about 20 yards apart from one another, with each one sitting in the heel position. Have the thrower positioned to throw the mark at a distance of about 50 yards. Attach your belt cord to the dog. When you are ready, signal for the mark to be thrown, and reinforce your dog's position by commanding "hup—stay." The other handler will send his dog to the mark. If your dog breaks, correct him with the belt cord as you did in his early training. If he stays, give him a little praise and reinforce his stay with another *hup—stay* command. After the other dog has returned and given up the bird, release your dog and praise him wildly. Then toss him a bumper or a dead bird for a quick and short retrieve. Now rerun the setup exactly as before. After the second rerun, do it again, only this time give your dog the retrieve and have the other handler's dog honor him.

After a few sessions, you can begin to dispense with the belt cord. If the dog should break (fail to honor), then you will need to chase him down and take him back to his spot to correct him for breaking, just as you did in the early training.

Be careful not to yell the dog's name if he breaks. Why? Because saying his name is telling him to retrieve, and that is not what you want him to be doing. A simple "no" will suffice.

After the dog is reliably honoring a single marked retrieve, have him honor for a double marked retrieve, and introduce gunshots when each of those marks is thrown. Do not be surprised if the dog breaks on either a gunshot or at the fall of the second mark. The reinforcement of the honor and the correction for a break will be no different than before. Even the best-trained dogs will break an honor from time to time, but if never trained to honor, it is likely that your dog will be a rather disrespectful fellow. Your dog's disrespect will not put you in good stead with your hunting buddies should your dog start stealing their dogs' retrieves.

Honoring in the field after another dog has flushed a bird is really only a matter of being steady to wing, shot, and fall. If your dog breaks, you need to get to him quickly and correct him as you would for any failure to remain steady in the field.

Teaching a dog to honor at the line or in the field is something that should not be overlooked if for no other reason than it is a courtesy to your friends and their dogs.

Hunting in Brace

Until the very last series of a spaniel field trial, all dogs are run as a brace (hunt tests do not require brace work); this is a reflection of how commonly braces are used when hunting pheasant or grouse every fall. When running as a brace, two dogs work a field together, with each dog covering his own sector of the field. A flush made by one dog is honored by his bracemate. Likewise, when one dog is sent to make a retrieve, his bracemate is honoring that retrieve even though the bird may have fallen closer to the bracemate than to the working dog.

Working in brace requires a dog to be steady to wing, shot, and fall, as well as to honor all work done by the other dog. Furthermore, it requires a dog to respect the other dog's sector of the field and be responsive to the owner's signals to turn from the edge of the bracemate's sector and return to

his own. As you may be able to tell from this description, running in brace is not a job for the poorly trained dog.

While this book is not meant to be an introduction to training your dog for field trials, that does not mean we cannot address brace work for the hunting dog. Because many hunting spaniel owners will hit the fields with friends of like mind who also own hunting spaniels, it is good to take some time to cover a few of the fine points.

The reason people usually want to run two dogs at a time is because two dogs can cover a large area more efficiently than one can. Theoretically, these hunters get more opportunities to find, flush, and shoot birds. Efficient coverage is not obtained by having the two dogs run side by side or near one another, but by having each dog cover his own area directly in front of his handler, just as he would do if the dog and handler were out hunting alone. That area in front of the handler then becomes the dog's sector of the field and his primary area of concentration. When a hunting brace is run, there are normally at least three hunters who spread out across a field and move through it in a relatively straight line, with the dog handlers on each end.

When working a field in brace, your dog works between an imaginary line (center line), which separates the two sectors, and the outside edge of his area. To keep your dog within his own area, you simply have him turn back into it as he approaches the center line by giving the *turn* whistle (*tweet-tweet*). Remember, you are hunting, not trialing, so you are not out to get extra points for style as much as you are to make sure that the work is efficient.

As for all of the honoring that occurs with brace work, this is something that you should always work on and that needs to be addressed in training. Once you feel that your dog is proficient at being steady at the line and in the field, you can begin to practice brace work with other spaniels. To do this, first establish a course through a field by marking a center line with either bicycle flags or surveyor's tape. Put two flags each at both the start point and the end point of the course, and set one flag about every 10 yards as you move from the start to finish point. If possible, have three gunners, and position them so that there is one in the middle, who will walk along the center line, one at the far right of the course, and one at the far left of the course. The dogs and their handlers are then set up to the right and left of the center gunner. Avoid planting or rolling in birds toward the center line when training, and alternate the birds so that you do not have birds flushing simultaneously on each side of the course.

From this point on, practicing brace work simply means controlling your dog's actions regarding honoring, steadiness, and turning on the whistle. If you practice this enough, you will find that the dog begins to spot the center gun and knows that, when he does, he should turn back and head the other way. In effect, the dog begins to work between the guns and so does not enter the other dog's sector. If a dog fails to honor his bracemate's flush or retrieve, the handler must get to the dog quickly and correct him for his failure, preferably before he interferes with the bracemate any further.

Running a brace can be fun, but it can also be very frustrating in the beginning. Remember that your dog is learning a new activity and will probably succumb to new temptations. Your early work with the dog and the foundation that you have built is all you need to overcome those problems and turn your dog into a courteous bracemate.

It's been a successful day for this owner and his two
Boykin Spaniels.

Chapter 9

Measuring Your Progress

It is often hard for you to know just how well you or your dog is doing without an objective third party to evaluate the dog's skills against a set standard. As owner, companion, and trainer, you are probably a bit less objective than you should be or perhaps a bit more critical than you need to be. You can probably find people willing to give you both criticism and training suggestions within your local field training club, or perhaps you can pay for such an evaluation by a professional trainer, but there are also other ways to measure your success.

The AKC's Spaniel Hunt Test Program

The American Kennel Club (AKC)'s spaniel hunt test program is a testing format designed to assess both natural and trained abilities through a series of three different test levels: Junior Hunter, Senior Hunter, and Master Hunter. Dogs are awarded titles representing the level of success that they have demonstrated. In all levels, dogs must demonstrate their ability to perform as upland flushing dogs and their

Spaniel hunt tests provide a concrete way to measure your dog's progress in the field.

willingness to complete at least one water retrieve. Each level is based on a set standard of performance, and judges must judge a dog based on that standard, taking into account the particular spaniel breed's hunting style. If you are looking for a way to measure your and your dog's success as you move through the training process, these hunt tests certainly are one means of doing so.

Each of the three test levels of the program has a specific set of criteria that must be met in order to pass, and a dog must pass each test level a specified number of times to earn the respective title.

Junior Hunter—Upland requirement: must find, flush, and have the opportunity to retrieve two birds on land. Water requirement: must be line steady and retrieve one bird to hand from the water at a distance of 20 to 25 yards with a shot fired. Title requirement: four passes to be awarded a title. (American Water Spaniels must also pass two Junior Hunter retrieving certification tests.)

Senior Hunter—Upland requirement: must find, flush, and retrieve two birds to hand on land. The dog must complete a hunt dead on land at a distance of 35 to 40 yards. Water requirement: must retrieve one bird from the water at a distance of 30 to 35 yards with a shot fired and must be line steady. Title requirement: if a dog has earned a Junior Hunter title, he must earn four passes to be awarded a Senior Hunter title. The dog that has not earned a Junior Hunter title must earn five passes to be awarded a Senior Hunter title. (American Water Spaniels must also pass two senior hunter retrieving certification tests.)

Master Hunter—Upland requirement: must find, flush, and retrieve two birds to hand on land and must demonstrate steadiness to wing and shot. The dog must complete a hunt dead on land at a distance of 55 to 60 yards. Water requirement: retrieve one bird from the water at a distance of 40 to 45 yards with a shot fired and complete a blind retrieve at a distance of 30 to 40 yards. The dog must be line steady at the water. Title requirement: if a dog has earned a Senior Hunter title, he must earn five passes to be awarded the Master Hunter title. The dog that has not earned a Senior Hunter title must earn six passes to be awarded a Master Hunter title. (American Water Spaniels must also pass two Master Hunter retrieving certification tests.)

The AKC spaniel hunt test program is available in many parts of the country. Those who participate have not only a good way of measuring their progress but also a form of incentive to drive them to achieve more with their dogs. In addition, participation in the program lets you meet others with similar interests who can serve as mentors, assist you in training,

and provide other elements of support toward meeting your objectives.

Determining Your Own Success

I have always been a pragmatist, looking at the reality of things rather than dreaming about what should be. As a spaniel breeder, trainer, and hunt test judge, I have a good understanding of how the ideal flushing spaniel should perform in the field. However, over the

It must smell like success to this English Springer Spaniel.

Participation in hunting events gives you the chance to connect with like-minded spaniel people.

This understanding makes it easier for me to accept that each of us has his own objectives and interests. The simple fact that yours may be different from mine in no way makes one better or more appropriate than the other; it simply makes them different.

If your training objectives fall somewhat short of obtaining what I believe to be a finished gundog, neither I nor anyone else—including yourself—should make you feel that you have in any way failed. You are responsible for setting your own goals, and you are the only one who can decide what you want or need in a gundog. Do not allow others to set your objectives for you or to decide what training method is best for meeting them. In fact, explore a variety of methods and choose for yourself, always keeping in mind that no matter what you do, you and your dog should be having fun.

I believe that a great way to end this book is to quote Steve Smith of the *Retriever Journal*, who offered this bit of wisdom: "So decide what skills your dog has to know, what ones you would like him to know, and what skills it would be nice for him to know but it's no big deal. Then, train for them in that order."

Enjoy the journey.

years I have also come to understand that not everyone wants or even needs the ideal dog to enjoy time afield and have a great relationship with a canine companion.

Bibliography

Bailey, Joan. *How To Help Gundogs Train Themselves*. Portland, OR: Swan Valley Press, 1992.

Brown, Bernie. *The No-force Method of Dog Training*. Galesburg, IL: H & S Publications, 1983.

Irving, Joe. *Gundogs, Their Learning Chain*, 2nd edition. Shropshire, UK: Swan Hill Press, 1998.

Quinn, Tom. *The Working Retrievers*. Guilford, CT: The Lyons Press, 1998.

Roebuck, Kenneth C. *Gun-Dog Training: Spaniels and Retrievers*. Mechanicsburg, PA: Stackpole Books, 1982.

Roettger, Anthony Z. and Benjamin H. Schleider III. *Urban Gundogs*. Cranston, RI: The Writer's Collective, 2005.

Spencer, James B. *HUP! Training Flushing Spaniels the American Way*. New York: Howell Book House, 1992.

———. *Retriever Training Drills for Blind Retrieves*. Crawford, CO: Alpine Publications, 2001.

———. *Training Retrievers for Marshes and Meadows*. Crawford, CO: Alpine Publications, 1998.

Tarrant, Bill. *Tarrant Trains Gundogs*. Mechanicsburg, PA: Stackpole Books, 1989.

Index

Index